EDUCATIONAL LEADERSHIP

A Guyanese Perspective

DR. BRIAN O'TOOLE

with a Foreword by PROFESSOR ROY MCCONKEY

Published by School of Nations, Guyana 2018

ISBN #: ISBN 978-976-8254-30-6 (Hardcover)

Copies can be ordered from:

Dr. Brian O'Toole, Director,

School of Nations,

41 New Market Street,

Georgetown, Guyana

otoole.nations@gmail.com

Design and layout by LuCa Design, www.lucadesign.ca

DEDICATION

To our grandchildren who have enriched
our lives in so many ways

Declan

Haydar

Matthew

Laylí

Anyssa

TABLE OF CONTENTS

ABBREVIATIONS

ABE	Association of Business Executives
AIB	Australian Institute of Business
AIFO	Amici do Raoul Follereau
BCHP	Bahá'í Community Health Partnership
CBR	Community Based Rehabilitation
CHW	Community Health Worker
CODE	Canadian Organisation for Development through Education
HFLE	Health and Family Life Education
IADB	Inter- American Development Bank
LBSA	Look Back Step Ahead
NU	Nations University
NURI	Nations Research Institute
NCA	Nancy Campbell Academy
NGO	Non Governmental Organisation
OWOW	On the Wings of Words
SON	School of Nations
UNDP	United Nations Development Programme
VF	Varqa Foundation
VHB	Village Health Board
VSO	Voluntary Service Organisation
YCMTW	Youth Can Move the World
WHO	World Health Organisation

Foreword

Emeritus Professor Roy McConkey, OBE, PhD. Ulster University, Northern Ireland and Visiting Professor, University of Cape Town

Many books have been written about leadership but few are like this one. Most have focussed on leadership in business or politics with their hierarchical structures and leaders at their pinnacle. But here you read of a different kind of leadership.

The focus is on leaders whose primary aim is to help communities to help themselves. Not directing, managing, telling and cajoling people what to do but listening, supporting, guiding and encouraging ordinary men and women to make the changes they want to make. In these pages, you are given many practical examples of how this style of leadership was put into practice in what many would consider to be impoverished communities in one of the poorest countries in the Western Hemisphere. The success stories recounted here, testify to the effectiveness of this approach; although Brian O'Toole would rightly give the credit to the people of Guyana because they were ones who turned despair into hope.

The word 'educational' is another clue to the uniqueness of this book. The book is not just about leadership in education – although impressive examples are given of this – it is about leadership that educates. We still have much to learn about how best to help people acquire new knowledge and skills; especially men and women living in urban townships and rural villages who have limited opportunities for learning. This book provides many examples of educational initiatives focussed on disability, early child development, literacy, health promotion and social problems. The approaches used contrast markedly with those found in most schools and colleges. The learning was based around practical applications of knowledge, the provision of culturally appropriate resource materials - such as locally produced video programmes - and training local people to become trainers of others in their community. The educational leadership promoted in Guyana brings to life Nelson Mandela's assertion that "education is the most powerful weapon we can use to change the world".

Inevitably, Brian and his colleagues had to be selective in the programmes they established. They wisely chose to focus on children, youth and young adults because the future of every nation depends on them. Yet often development programmes are driven by adults and their priorities. The present-day needs of children are frequently overlooked. But as Mahatma Ghandi observed: "If we are to reach real peace in this world... we shall have to begin with children." Peace to grow and develop free from illness or disability; the peace of having the best education going and the peace that comes from a community that is confident and concerned for all its members. Guyana has shown that this is possible, even if it was only for some rather than most youth.

There is another dimension to the leadership described in this book that is worth highlighting; namely it is rooted in moral principles and values. As Martin Luther King wisely observed: "education without morals is like a ship without a compass, merely wandering nowhere". Brian came to

Guyana with strong personal convictions and he makes no apology for basing his work on them, nor should he. Over the 40 and more years he has spent in his adopted country, these values have been confirmed and strengthened through sharing his life and faith with the many thousands of people who have been involved in the programmes you will read about in this book. Hence we might extend King's analogy to say that morals are also the engine that brings the ship speedily to port.

It has been my privilege to visit Guyana many times over 20 years and experience at first-hand the various programmes that Brian instigated. It was an adventure in more ways than one; as we rode in bullock carts, speed boats and car ferries which were long-past their sell-by date, to visit remote coastal and inland villages. However these inconveniences were soon forgotten as I heard from enthusiastic participants about the programmes and saw the difference they were making to people's lives. Of course their journey was not all smooth sailing. Jealousies, competing priorities, personnel shortages and lack of funds had to be managed as they rarely could be avoided. Yet through this book, the insights gained from Guyana are now available to a wider readership nationally and globally.

Robert Frost, the American poet, imagines in a poem two roads diverging in a wood and by choosing to take the less travelled road, 'can make all the difference'. It takes both bravery and bravado to take a less travelled road – two attributes that are the hallmark of Brian O'Toole - and this book is testimony that it did make all the difference. I suspect though, many readers- myself included – will be left pondering if we would make the same choice, even knowing of the difference it can make. I hope you do.

A Journey of Faith

Brian O'Toole

ARRIVAL IN GUYANA

In 1978, I had qualified as an Educational Psychologist in Glasgow, Scotland which was where I met my future wife, Pam. I had been married for 10 days when I then set off alone to Guyana in search of employment with Pam following me once I had secured a job and a place to live. I left the UK for Guyana to assist with the Bahá'í Faith there, not as a missionary, as that is not a part of the Bahá'í Faith, rather to be simply of service to the community there. But, when I arrived in June 1978 I had no idea my wife and I would still be there almost 40 years later.

I began knocking on doors in search of employment in Guyana. Three months later I was given a job, teaching Psychology for 22 hours per week at the Teacher Training College to 325 students. It however took 32 visits to the Ministry of Education to secure that post as time-after-time I was told to 'come back later'.

The Guyana my wife and I arrived in was a curious mixture of warmth, hospitality, joy, kindness but also there was a profound sense of hopelessness and despair. Almost every conversation with the Guyanese people in those early days was about getting out of Guyana and securing a visa (legally or otherwise) for Canada or America. Such was the obsession about leaving that people, from all walks of life, were prepared to pay significant sums to 'buy' visas. The Visa Consular Officer at the US embassy was later convicted and imprisoned for obtaining huge sums of money in return for visas. The Canadian High Commission had to close its visa department in Guyana because of a 'sex for visas' scandal. Years later when Pam and I applied for Guyana citizenship the official at the Ministry of Foreign Affairs asked what had we done in UK to run away to Guyana

The newly-acquired Bahá'í Center in Edinburgh, Scotland, was the scene Saturday, June 10, of the first Bahá'í wedding ever to take place in Scotland without a civil ceremony. The bride is Pamela McClure, the groom Brian O'Toole. Both are from Glasgow. The wedding officer, one of three Bahá'ís in Scotland authorized to carry out weddings, was Surgeon Commander John More Nisbet of Edinburgh. Since this was the first non-Christian or non-Jewish marriage ceremony to be recognized in Scotland, news of it was published in one national, two Scottish and one local newspaper. BBC Radio-Scotland even recorded and broadcast a part of the ceremony and gave an accurate outline of the Faith. Three weeks after the wedding Brian O'Toole pioneered to Guyana where he soon was joined by his wife.

First Official Bahá'í Wedding in Scotland

Wedding day, with my parents, ten days before leaving for Guyana

to seek citizenship. Even an official at the Ministry of Foreign Affairs could not believe someone from UK would actually want to become Guyanese.

Guyana had recently become independent and there were many scars in those early days of post colonialism. The secretary of the senior Ministry of Education official who was handling my employment application, informed me that her boss had experienced prejudice in her time in UK and this was her way of redressing that balance.

Not long after arrival, Pam and I were at a social function with a group of 'ex pats' when the room went very quiet following the announcement that there had been a mass suicide in the interior of Guyana. Shortly after we learnt about Jonestown and the loss of 900 lives at the hands of a religious fanatic from the US who had sought out Guyana as the 'new Jerusalem' for his flock of lost parishioners from California. Days later my wife visited the Georgetown prison to meet with one of the very few persons who had survived the massacre. He had been ordered by Jim Jones to travel to the capital from their jungle base to kill the members of the Jonestown basketball team who happened to be in the city at that time for a game. He asked my wife simply if it was true that 900 had died.

It was also a time of physical insecurity. Many communities, including our own, chose to establish vigilante teams. I would be given my schedule each week to walk up and down the roads in our neighbourhood 'on guard' with a handful of neighbours. One night, three of us were walking with our cutlasses in hand when suddenly a young man jumped out from behind a bush to attack us. My 'companions' ran off and, without thinking, I was just about to strike the attacker with my cutlass. Suddenly I was hit with the irony that I was in Guyana to help develop the Bahá'í community only to cut the head off an assailant. I was however saved that prompting of conscience when it turned out that it was one of the other vigilante team members just having a bit of fun to lighten the boredom of the patrol. About an hour later my brave companions returned and said they 'had being going for help.'

It was a time when the autocratic leader of the country effectively banned all imports of food leading to sardines becoming a prized smuggled commodity. Flour was banned and was secretly taken into homes in the middle of the night. If the banned substance was found in your car – the car was confiscated. Pam herself was "arrested" along with a friend, or 'accomplice', late one night on her way home overland from neighbouring Suriname. I was to meet her in a town midway on the journey home. That was at the time that there were very few phones in Guyana. We went 20 years before we had our own phone. I travelled to the appointed rendezvous and she was not there. Unaware that she was in the police station for 'attempting to smuggle' two tins of tomato paste, a can of corned beef and a bar of chocolate into the country. Several hours later, after a full and frank 'written confession' she was released with assurances that the 'banned items will be destroyed' and was generously given the offer by her captor to go for a drink at the local rum shop – which was graciously declined. All of this only after frantic hours of my searching for her, blissfully unaware that she was a newly discovered felon. J.M. Synge, one of Ireland's playwrights talks about there being a world of difference 'between a gallous story and a dirty deed.' That dirty deed has now become a gallous story to tell at cocktail parties but at the time the humour of the incident was lost.

BAHÁ'Í FAITH

But thankfully that was not the only Guyana that we met. Through our work with the Bahá'í community, Pam and I stayed, with complete strangers in literally hundreds of villages throughout both the coast and interior of the country. Neither of us had ever experienced such uncomplicated acts of kindness, hospitality and generosity. Every weekend we took part in public meetings about the Bahá'í Faith, each attended by a minimum of 200 or 300 persons. Along with a small cadre of dedicated others, we did this for our first decade in Guyana. After ten years, 57,000 persons in Guyana had accepted the Bahá'í Faith, which at more than 7% of the population constituted the highest percentage of Bahá'ís in any mainland country in the world. Over the next 10 to 15 years that number shrank considerably as thousands and thousands of these new Bahá'ís, along with their compatriots, sought new lives in Toronto and New York.

Much of this book reflects on our attempts to put the fine principles of the Bahá'í Faith into practice. If so many people accepted a new Faith and nothing changed, what would be the purpose of such actions? We sought in programmes of literacy, child labour, basic education, youth leadership and work with persons of disabilities to see if the vision of the Bahá'í Faith could be translated into development projects that could really begin to impact peoples' lives. The following chapters try to analyse this process and see if there are lessons to be learnt.

Before travelling to Guyana I had the opportunity to travel in about 30 different countries throughout the world. I had spent a year in Africa and India looking for a place to live. The purpose for the move from the UK was the desire to be of service to the Bahá'í community that I had joined when I was 17 years old. In the Bahá'í Faith there is no clergy, no missionaries. If someone feels moved to travel to a new country he or she would need to find a job, become financially independent, and then see how to be of assistance to that community. My wife, Pamela, had also joined the Bahá'í Faith a few months before.

The Bahá'í Faith is an independent world religion that believes that God has sent different Messengers to mankind throughout history, in the form of Buddha, Zoroaster, Krishna, Jesus Christ and Muhamad and that about 150 years ago the Bahá'ís believe that God had sent another Messenger, Bahá'u'lláh, to bring about the unity of mankind.

Guyana proved to be a remarkably receptive land to the teachings of the Bahá'í Faith. For many Guyanese with a long tradition of Hinduism, Islam and Christianity it was not difficult to accept that another Messenger had come from God.

But as the numbers grew, the challenge then became what did it mean to say that 7% of the population was Bahá'í. If things did not change in their communities, what was the point of gathering more and more declarations of Faith? This reflection resulted in the stories that we relate in these pages of our efforts to translate the fine principles of the Bahá'í Faith into practical reality. Could we begin to articulate a new vision of leadership, community participation, empowerment, collaboration? Could we translate those fine words, that are replete in the development literature, into reality? In the process would it be possible to develop new lines of collaboration between ourselves from the North and peoples of the South that would see both parties enriched and move away from a model where the South tries to blindly imitate the North.

Indeed, the North-South partnership has provided much of the inspiration for this book. I had no intention to write a book. It was Professor Roy McConkey who suggested that there may be merit for such a publication. Roy has made more than 12 trips to Guyana over a period of two decades to help inspire us in our various endeavours. Despite his illustrious background as an internationally recognised writer, academic and leader in the disability field, he came to Guyana not as a 'Western expert' but as a true and humble partner. The accompaniment he provided, the example of service to the community he offered and the brilliance of his vision are at the heart of the various efforts featured in this book. Roy has been an invaluable contributor to this book on so many different levels. We owe Roy a great debt, he has enriched many of the lives featured in this book in fundamental ways.

It is all too easy however, forty years later, to look backwards and tell a coherent story as if it was based on a preconceived plan. The truth is of course very different. For whatever successes that are shared in these pages, there were as many false starts, obstacles, scenes of disunity and times of deep discouragement and disillusionment as some of the very people closest to us saw things in very different ways.

The joys as grandparents

So what is the purpose of this book? This book is intended as a reflection on the efforts made by a number of remarkable people to put faith into action and to begin to articulate some new lines of development. In particular it tries to document the key contributions of a number of remarkable persons from the North; Roy McConkey, Gordon Naylor, Pat Cameron, Jamshid Aidun, and Soma Stout in developing this course of action. Each played a far greater role in the process than they might imagine or admit to.

In this book Roy McConkey reflects on our collaboration, over a twenty year period, in developing the Guyana Community Based Rehabilitation programme from a small pilot project in a few villages to a nationwide undertaking that trained thousands of persons, and attracted visitors from many parts of the world and which led to more than 30 articles in international journals and two books on disability. This chapter includes insights from Juliet Solomon, from Trinidad, who served the programme with such distinction for many years.

Mrs. Pat Cameron, a gifted educator from Canada, came and assisted the 'On the Wings of Words' (OWOW) literacy programme on eight occasions. Pat shares her insights in the chapter on OWOW.

Gordon Naylor, the Principal of Nancy Campbell Academy (NCA) in Canada, the sister school to School of Nations in Guyana, was a fellow traveller on this journey. He and his family arrived in Guyana, from Canada, days after our own arrival and we worked very closely together for seven years on a variety of education projects. In returning to Canada he developed NCA into one of the top schools in Ontario. Gordon is also a pioneer in the area of the arts. He brought several teams of youth to School of Nations to explore how the performing arts can begin to help transform the concept of education.

Somava Stout came to Guyana twenty years ago as a graduate student from the University of Berkley to gather data for her Masters thesis which was based on both the Community Based Rehabilitation Programme and the Bahá'í Community Health Partnership, based in the Rupununi. That early visit was the first of many visits to Guyana. The fruits of that early pioneering work have contributed to the development of the 100 Million Healthier Lives programme that Somava helps to direct at the University of Harvard. The seeds sown early on in Rupununi are now germinating in the partnership that Nations has formed with IHI whereby the 6th Form students base their service project on the IHI programme.

Another chapter explores the youth leadership programme, Youth Can Move the World, which attracted youth from literally every corner of the country to work as volunteers in their villages; working with other youth on topics such as, domestic violence, protection of the environment, HIV/ AIDs and suicide prevention. The two remarkable coordinators, Rosheni Takechandra and Lomeharshan Lall offer their insights in this chapter.

The chapter on Integrated Development in the Rupununi, a native Amerindian area on the border with Brazil, includes inputs from Dr. Jamshid Aidun and Ms. Lorraine Pierre. Dr. Aidun volunteered for 12 years as the only doctor in the entire region. Lorraine, herself an Amerindian, was our guide and mentor on all our journeys into the interior. The chapter documents the way that a traditional medical outreach programme grew into an integrated development project that touched the lives of everyone living in the entire region.

The contribution by Othneil Lewis, the Chairman of the 6th Form Student Council at School of Nations, explores what empowerment might look like in practice. Othneil's chapter looks at the response of a group of 6th Formers at Nations to the imposition of a 14% VAT tax on Private Education that was recently imposed by the government. It traces the way they effectively took on the government to revoke the tax by articles in the paper and appearances on TV and radio and the organisation of a petition, signed by more than 15,000 persons (more than 2% of the population) opposing the tax. It also traces their victory in this campaign.

I would like to record my sincere thanks to my daughter-in-law, Lua O'Toole and her company LuCa design for the magic of her skills in graphic design that have transformed a printed page into a mosaic of special moments. We also thank Mensah Fox and his company for printing this book in record time.

Dr. Ian McDonald, one of Guyana's leading literary figures, gave a comprehensive and very helpful critique of an early copy of the book. Just when I thought I had finished the book Ian met me for two hours and provided invaluable feedback which resulted in extensive re-writing.

But there would have been no book, no journey, were it not for the contribution of my wife of forty years. Pam and I married just 10 days before I left for Guyana to find employment. Pam was a newly qualified primary school teacher. She had only once left UK and that for a brief holiday in Spain. People warned me she might not be able to 'adjust to Guyana'. But from her first day she fell in love with her new home and its people and she totally embraced a new lifestyle that was to enrich both our lives and which would give our two boys, who spent the first 16 years of their lives in Guyana, an understanding of what unity in diversity could look like.

This book attempts to reflect on what lessons can be learnt from a range of grass roots, modestly funded, educational endeavours in the areas of disability, literacy, child labour, education, cultural affirmation and integrated development and to see if these efforts might have wider applicability.

The world of development has its own vocabulary. The word 'sustainability' is one catchword of all development initiatives. Sustainability within impoverished economies is however a daunting prospect. Despite the 'success' of the Guyana CBR programme a later chapter in this book reflects on what did the government do, or not do, to enrich and expand the initiative. As mentioned in the chapter on Community Based Rehabilitation, there have been very few, if any, CBR initiatives that have gone on and flourished into national programmes funded by host governments.

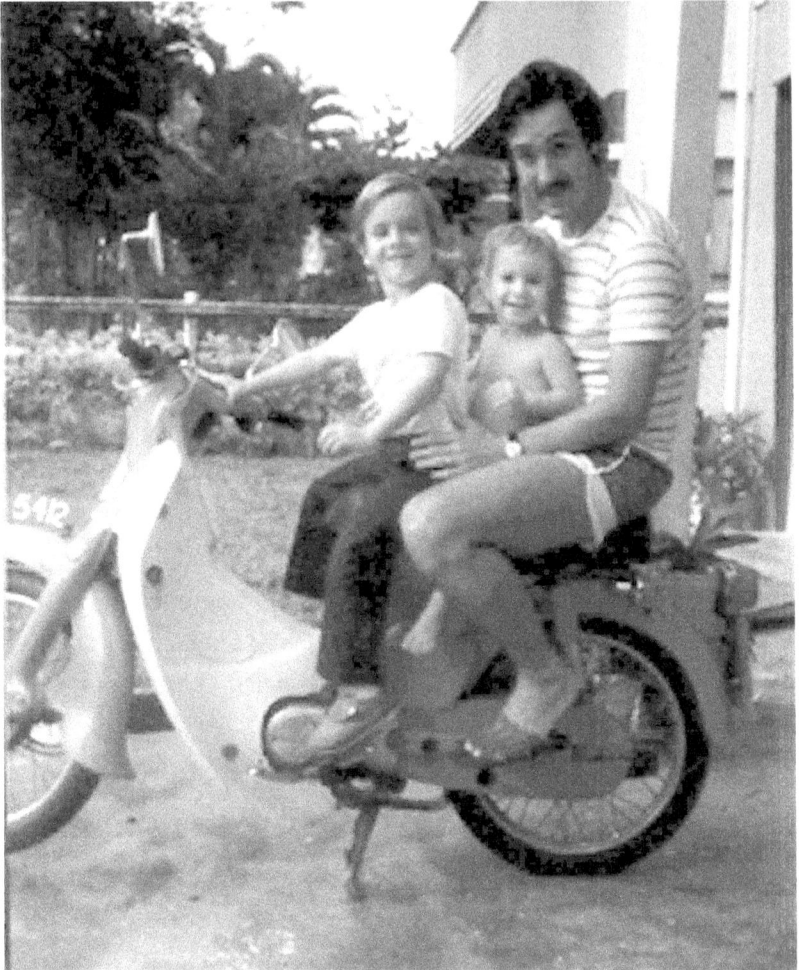

Early days in Guyana

The chapter on two decades work of the youth leadership programme, Youth Can Move the World, speaks about how a small grassroots programme that emerged out of a series of consultations in isolated villages in the interior of Guyana grew, over a 20-year period, into a programme that touched the lives of 8,000 youth in every corner of Guyana. That chapter in this book asks, what of that programme now?

There have been decades of international failures in the area of literacy. The then Minister of Education in Guyana lauded the 'On the Wings of Words' programme as 'the most effective path to literacy in Guyana'. This book also features a chapter on this programme and questions why there has not been greater government support for this programme.

The catalyst for my wife and I to begin our own school, School of Nations, was two-fold. Firstly, we were exhausted listening to our two boys, who were attending one of the best schools in the country, relate every evening at dinner that they had one, two, three, or more missed subjects that day. Secondly, there was a desire for us to introduce a programme over which we had more control. The catalyst for this was a chance visit I made, during a UN consultancy I was undertaking in West Africa, to a school in Lome, Togoland that was run by a young Bahá'í couple. That school was an oasis of peace in a troubled land. That visit was in April 1998, by August of that year we had opened School of Nations with classes from Nursery to 4th Form. Of all the innovations explored in this book Pam and I have/had the greatest control over is, of course, School of Nations and Nations University. We try and explore the significance of this in the chapters that follow.

Whilst writing this book we were informed that one of our students was placed first out of 13,000 students in the entire country in the Primary School 'Common Entrance' examination. Three years after starting Nations, we read in a Ministry of Education report that Nations was ranked second in the country in terms of Secondary School examination results. The first place went to a school with a 150-year head start.

From that uncertain beginning in 1998, School of Nations has now grown to a community of 3,000 persons with Pre-School, Nursery, Primary, Special Unit, Secondary and 6th Form Departments, and a pro bono school in a rural area. Also tertiary education is provided through Nations University in partnerships with the Universities of Cambridge, London and Bedfordshire and programmes offered in collaboration with the Association of Business Executives (ABE) and the Project Management Institute (PMI).

Branches of Nations have now opened in three other rural areas. A partnership has been formed with Brain Rx in Colorado, USA to provide special education training at Nations. Nations has been approached by

Cambridge International Examinations to become an 'Associate School' responsible for the entire Caribbean region. Nations has therefore offered us an opportunity to work largely independently of the government system and thereby explore our version of sustainability.

For every success that the following chapters may suggest, there could be as many additional pages on the frustrations faced, the disunity encountered, the prejudices to overcome and the sad apathy and disinterest on the parts of those in authority.

The final chapter of this book therefore attempts to see if there are key lessons that can be learnt from the various initiatives outlined that might offer insights to others in the area of education and development.

This book is on 'Educational Leadership' but it has adopted a broad definition of 'education' and 'leadership.' A number of the examples used in the book are drawn, not just from innovations in education, but from socio-economic development projects in health, youth leadership, HIV/AIDs and primary health care. In reflecting on 'leadership' it looks at models of moral leadership and examines the key ingredients necessary to bring about meaningful change.

BACKGROUND INFORMATION ON GUYANA

With a 459-kilometre Atlantic coastline on the northeast shoulder of the south American continent, Guyana is bounded by Venezuela on the west, Brazil on the west and south, and Suriname on the east. In 2016 the population was estimated to be below 700,000. Remarkably when we arrived in Guyana forty years ago this was the same figure. Guyana has an ethnic mix of peoples from African, Indian, Chinese, European and native Amerindian backgrounds. The coastal plain, which occupies about 5 percent of the country's area, is home to more than 90 percent of its inhabitants.

Much of the interior highlands consist of grassland. The largest expanse of grassland, the Rupununi Savannah, covers about 15,000 square kilometers in southern Guyana. The sparse grasses of the savannah in general support only grazing.

The UNDP's Human Development Report of 2014 (UNDP, 2014), ranked Guyana in 121st position out of 187 countries. Guyana has stagnated in the same ranking position since 2008. UNICEF (2016) estimated that around 422,000 Guyanese live in other countries. They have been driven away by the lack of economic opportunities at home. This brain drain creates losses of around 8% of the country's GDP and emigration disunites families and forces children to live far from one or both parents. It has been widely quoted in the media that each year 85% of those who graduate from the University of Guyana leave for North America.

Guyana has long been the third poorest country in the Western Hemisphere, after Haiti and Nicaragua. Unemployment is high, and it is particularly acute for youth who represent more than 60% of Guyana's population.

Guyana's latest official poverty measurement was done in 2006, prior to the economic crisis that hit the world in 2008. According to that measure, 36% of the population was living in poverty.

In terms of health, few of the indicators are positive. Maternal mortality estimates for 2015 stand at 229/100,000 live births, a number that has not shown significant progress since the year 2000. Child mortality numbers also have shown only small reductions since the year 2000.

Neonatal mortality continues to be the major component of under-5 mortality in the country. This is Influenced by inadequate health care, lack of full immunization, poor water and sanitation, and by household food insecurity.

Guyana has the second highest incidence, after Haiti, of HIV/ AIDS in the Caribbean and AIDS is considered the second leading cause of death in the country. Most of the new cases of HIV/AIDs are found among 15 and 19 year old boys and girls. Knowledge is one of the most important components in avoiding HIV transmission. Less than half of the adolescent population between 15 and 19 years of age have comprehensive knowledge on HIV and AIDS.

The picture is not very different in terms of education. Boys and girls are dropping out of school for a variety of reasons. The country's economic situation pushes some of them to leave school early without the necessary qualification and then taking low paid jobs. Many do not see the benefits of continuing their academic studies and for others, their education ends prematurely because of pregnancy. UNICEF estimated that more than 40% of the youth in Guyana are unemployed

Children living in single-parent households, especially those headed by women constitute another group of vulnerable children. These family arrangements are driven by the harsh economic situation that pushes parents, mainly men, to search for jobs abroad or in the most remote areas of the country in mining and logging.

However, the picture is changing dramatically as now Guyana has recorded one of the biggest oil finds in recent history. The economy, which has long been reliant on rice, sugar and bauxite is now poised for a fundamental transformation. Educational Leadership will surely play a major role in whether Guyana now moves out of the impoverishment of previous decades.

CHAPTER 1

Community Based Rehabilitation: Some Lessons From Guyana

Brian O'Toole

THE CALL TO ACTION

We had been living in Guyana for five years, when a neighbour came to my house and asked for help. I had known the family for several years since coming to live in a semi-rural area some 10 kilometres from Georgetown but separated by a wide river estuary and crossed by the world's longest floating bridge which closed frequently for repairs. Our children played together, but I had no idea that there was another child in that family who never went out of her house. Her name was Nalini, she was a severely handicapped teenager.

We lived only a few miles from a modern rehabilitation centre. Nalini's mum had visited the centre a few times, but now her daughter was simply too big to be carried on and off the public transportation needed to get there. We therefore formed a small group to see if there was anything we could do to help this family. Later we were to discover that there were in fact thousands of other families in Guyana in the same situation.

We are now in a new century far away from that early encounter in 1978. But we can reflect on how future historians might characterise the last five decades of development initiatives. Will these years be seen to be replete with rhetoric in slogans, reports, declarations but that have brought few improvements to the world's poorest people? Or will the seeds have been sown of new innovations that will allow the record to be balanced with a new model of service delivery? In the field of rehabilitation will we simply have conservatively followed outworn traditions or will we be seen to have articulated a new model of service delivery?

We could debate the precise number of disabled persons in need of help in Guyana and internationally. What is clear however is that a disproportionate number of the world's disabled population live in developing countries. As long as poverty, malnutrition, conflict, war and superstition plague much of the world, the numbers will continue to rise. The overwhelming majority of persons with disabilities, like Nalini, will pass their lives without dignity, in absolute poverty, victimised by beliefs that they are possessed by evil spirits or that their very existence is proof of divine punishment.

The typical response to disability internationally is shame, prejudice and exclusion from community life. The fine words from Article 23 of the UN Convention of the Rights of the Child are yet to permeate most societies. " …. a mentally or physically disabled child should enjoy a full and decent life in conditions which ensure dignity, promote self-reliance and facilitate the child's active participation in the community."

This chapter aims to explore the impact of an alternative service provision for persons with disabilities in Guyana and to examine whether there may be lessons to be learnt from this experience for other countries.

CHILDREN WITH SPECIAL NEEDS IN GUYANA

In 1978 Guyana had only one special school in the capital and this was for children with hearing impairments and intellectual disabilities. There was a waiting list to enter the school. There was also one centre for children with physical disabilities and a unit for children with visual impairments attached to a local school. There were also two, very small, units for a total of twenty children with special needs in two rural towns. The capital with 23% of the population of the county therefore had more than 90% of the provision in the area of Special Education. Forty years later however the situation has hardly changed. The gap between need and available services is therefore painfully obvious.

Guyana does not have a reliable measure of how many children with special needs there are in the country, or how many are in need of formal education. Small-scale surveys have identified that 15% of all persons with disabilities have never attended school, and the proportion increases to 42% among children younger than 16 years of age. The educational system is ill-equipped to include children with sensory, cognitive, and/or mental impairments. Hence the majority of children with disabilities stay at home, resulting in isolation, and stigmatization. They have difficulties in accessing not only schools, but also health services, employment and even social and recreational opportunities.

A major reason for the lack of progress in addressing the needs of children with disabilities has been the widespread adoption globally of inappropriate models of service delivery. As Arbab (1984) said, "we have been seduced by a modernisation mirage which has fostered the illusion that western skills, knowledge and attitudes should be diffused to people in developing countries." In our blinkered desire to imitate a western style of service provision we have lost sight of the true magnitude of the problem. Where services do exist, as in Guyana, they have been modelled on those found in more affluent countries, characterised by specialist, segregated provision located in the major towns with the vast majority of persons in rural areas being totally neglected.

The justification for this focus has been the need to 'maintain standards', however to the 98% of families who are presently receiving no help, the arguments over standards has no relevance. We need to remind ourselves that the vast majority of humankind are villagers who live in rural communities that until very recently, with the advent of the internet and other widely accessible forms of communicating, had not changed in hundreds of years and which remained totally unaware of the slogans and declarations being voiced on their behalf.

As Miles (1985) said: "the cries of the oppressed filter through as bloodless statistics...while the response trickles back as theoretical programmes."

No nation can morally or practically ignore a problem affecting such numbers of its citizens. More economical approaches will have to be explored to meet the magnitude of the challenge. Innovative models need to be found to make rehabilitation services relevant and accessible to rural peoples. We need a reappraisal of the concept of staffing, the model of training they receive and the nature of services offered by them. A new role needs to be played by rehabilitation therapists as promoters of community development.

The United Nations has taken a lead in this respect with the UN Declaration of Human Rights and the UN Convention on the Rights of Persons with Disabilities (UNCRPD) which articulate a human rights model and a radical move away from the outworn charity models and medical based responses to disability that have dominated across the world. The challenge now is to translate such sentiments into action.

RESPONSE TO THE CHALLENGE: COMMUNITY BASED REHABILITATION

In my early years in Guyana, I taught Psychology at the Teacher Training College and worked as a volunteer in the unit for children with physical disabilities at the Pediatric Clinic at the Public Hospital in the capital.   In the hospital I wrote erudite reports on children with special needs which promptly gathered dust on the shelves and were neither read nor actioned by other hospital colleagues or community services.

In 1981, I had the opportunity to go to Jamaica for the Caribbean Conference of Rehabilitation Therapists and heard a presentation by Padmani Mendis, one of the architects of the World Health Organisation's new approach to disability services called 'Community Based Rehabilitation' but widely termed 'CBR'. I was at once attracted to the philosophy as outlined by Padmani and, at the same time, fascinated by the depth of opposition her approach attracted from the audience of rehabilitation therapists. They felt their turf was being taken away from them as community services, rather than specialist clinics and centres, were seen as the future.

This initial interest expanded over the next several years into the topic of my PhD research programme at the Institute of Education of London University. Having worked in the field of disability in Guyana for several years I was well aware that the existing approach was only addressing a fraction of the need. At the same time however I was intrigued by the manner in which WHO was introducing CBR as *the* solution to the challenge. I wanted to review the available research internationally and undertake an empirical study to evaluate the claims made by the WHO for this new approach to disability.

Community Based Rehabilitation (CBR) aimed to bridge the gap between unmet needs and affordable service provision. CBR advocates the use of simplified methods of rehabilitation and the promotion of awareness and responsibility in the family and the wider community. The major goal of CBR is to train a new cadre of workers from the community, whether they be Community Health Workers, Teachers, Social Workers or volunteers who would then work alongside someone in the child's home to assist with the child.

CBR is an attempt to generate an exponential increase in appropriate skills and distribute them to where the needs are by utilizing hitherto unexploited resources in the community. The basic premise of CBR is that the greatest resource in developing countries for helping persons with disabilities lead lives which are fulfilled and productive, is a well advised and supported family. The goal therefore seeks for rehabilitation to become part of community development whereby the community seeks to improve itself. I was immediately attracted by the vision outlined by Padmani. When she spoke of her CBR experience in countries in Africa and Asia, with poorly developed special education facilities and modest health and social service provision, I felt I could have been listening to a description of Guyana. But whilst the philosophy was immediately attractive, I also felt rather uneasy about the way the innovation was being presented as *the* solution rather than an approach to be explored. This proved to be the catalyst for my desire to try and research the strengths and limitations of the approach within a Guyanese context.

The philosophy of CBR is immediately attractive and persuasive but can it be translated into practice? Do parents welcome a teaching or training role with their child? Is community involvement in this area realistic? Are there persons in rural villages who wish to offer their services in such a programme? The 'Hopeful Steps' CBR programme in Guyana attempted to offer responses to these questions but equally we needed evidence that would convince governments to invest in these new approaches.

HOPEFUL STEPS: THE GUYANA CBR PROGRAMME

The vision we had for 'Hopeful Steps' had to be translated into action but to do so, even on a small scale, needed money. Donor funding was sought to cover the expense. We knew, from previous experience, that government monies would not be available. The project was funded in the first two years by Action on Disability and Development from UK and then for the next decade, the European Union and an Italian NGO, Amici di Raoul Follereau (AIFO), were the funders. The funding covered training costs, materials, travel and teaching supplies, and later salaries for the National and Regional coordinators to support the community volunteers. Hopeful Steps began with a series of meetings with officials from the Ministries of Health and Education to share the philosophy of CBR and to try to engage them in initial discussions on the merits of this new approach. They were supportive of these new ideas and were willing to help explore whether the philosophy could be translated into practice in a Guyanese context. We began with a systematic survey by a number of trained volunteers of 4,500 persons in one coastal village in Guyana. About 1.5% of children and adults in that population were found to be in need of special help for their disability. We chose to launch the CBR project there for a number of reasons. It had a history of community involvement, it was a rural location but within easy reach of the capital where most of the resources were located and the survey had raised expectations that help would be forthcoming.

There followed a series of radio programmes, newspaper articles and announcements in schools, health clinics and places of worship to lay the foundation for the CBR programme. A public meeting to introduce the programme, 'Hopeful Steps', was chaired by the Mayor and attended by 200 persons. Nalini's mother was one of those in attendance. Sixty persons offered to be trained as volunteers. It was however made clear at the outset that there was no prospect of employment and there would be no payment for participating. Finally, 26 persons were accepted as volunteers from a wide variety of backgrounds including; nursing, teaching, social work, students, housewives and parents of children with disabilities.

GETTING STARTED

The volunteers met twice per week to undertake the 150-hour training in CBR to learn ways that they could help children with disabilities. The training was provided mainly by myself and by Geraldine Maison-Halls, a senior Physiotherapist, and the co-coordinator of the programme. Geraldine played a key role throughout the programme. She was one of a small team of persons internationally who had been identified by WHO as resource persons for CBR, she is also a gifted physiotherapist in her own right and she is a very creative trainer. Our partnership proved vital in gaining acceptance for the programme.

We also arranged for as many of the limited number of rehabilitation professionals that we had working in Guyana to be involved in the training. In part, the objective here was to pre-empt potential opposition from the rehabilitation 'experts' by giving them a sense of involvement in the programme.

The training followed the WHO recommended outline for CBR training as outlined by Helander et al (1989). Topics covered included; introduction to various disabilities, assessment of disability, child development, importance of play, making toys, puppet making, teaching ideas, assessing the progress of the child, ways of interacting with family members and the wider community, community education and the challenge of inclusive education.

Sessions were held in a local school, two evenings per week for 30 weeks and aimed to share knowledge, change attitudes and impart skills. The teaching sessions were interactive with extensive use of role play, videos and demonstrations. The two CBR coordinators then accompanied the volunteers as they worked with the families in their homes. This 'accompaniment' was a key ingredient in maintaining the interest, commitment and enthusiasm of the volunteers. Unlike many similar programmes in other countries, the drop-out rate for the volunteers was very low. Only three of the volunteers did not complete the programme.

Each volunteer had identified children with a disability in their neighbourhood and during the training they worked with one or two children and their families. In each home, a family member was identified who would work alongside the child. The volunteers would suggest certain activities to this family member who would then help the child learn new skills.

Hopeful Steps began with a focus on children, and later as the children grew older, the focus was expanded to include the challenge of working with youth and adults with disabilities. Essential to the new focus on adults was Income Generation projects aimed to help move the families out of poverty.

REHABILITATION COMMITTEE

The majority of volunteers became deeply involved in the CBR project and a sense of belonging soon emerged as they came to regard the programme as their own. A Rehabilitation Committee was formed which gradually took responsibility for the programme in the villages. The members of the committee were elected from the volunteers and family members involved in the pilot project.

As the home visits continued, the Committee approached the local Hindu organisation in one of the villages to create a Resource Unit for children with disabilities who were unable to attend regular schools. The Ministry of Education seconded the Head Teacher and two other teachers to work in this unit. All three were CBR graduates. Eight years later the community still managed the Resource Centre. Hence a key feature of 'Hopeful Steps' from the outset was the involvement of the wider community in the organisation and management of the programme in their locality.

EXPANDING THE PROGRAMME

The success of the CBR programme in the first village encouraged its spread to other locations and the development of other initiatives. Over the next 15 years, 'Hopeful Steps' expanded into every region of the country, including the remote interior region of the Rupununi. In each one, up to three times as many persons applied to be accepted as volunteers on the programme as could be accommodated. The dropout rate over the 12 to 15 months of each of the trainings was never more than 5%. When asked about their motivation they simply stated that they "wanted to be of service to their communities". The role of the volunteers became clearer as we learnt from their experiences about the impact they had on families. Their key functions were to; devise training programmes, give advice, offer support and counselling to the children and their families, obtain equipment and aids and promote social integration. Over the next 15 years I had the opportunity to undertake CBR consultancies and evaluations in more than 30 countries. In none of these countries were volunteers raised from the community in the manner they were in Guyana. In four visits to Ghana for example the 'volunteers' from isolated rural communities asked me directly "What will I be given for participating?" Not once in 15 years was I asked that question in Guyana.

DEVELOPMENT OF TRAINING MATERIALS

The need for locally produced training materials became clear early on. Volunteers learn by seeing and doing rather than via lectures and textbooks. They wanted practical information which they could relate to and apply to their own situation. Video programmes were filmed in local village settings thereby reflecting the viewer's world. This resulted in ready-made training materials which could then be used in outlying areas where it is often difficult to get the scarce professionals to visit.

The first video training course, 'Step by Step', helped volunteers to assess the needs of the child and then develop appropriate teaching ideas. The materials helped to explore what the child can do already and examine what the next appropriate step should be to focus on, and then to select appropriate teaching ideas and help the child progress to higher levels of development. The video training package included; assessment sheets, the steps a child goes through in learning certain key skills, teaching ideas, suggestions to achieve each of the steps on the assessment sheet, a 20-minute video on each theme, and video record worksheets to encourage people not to simply watch the videos passively.

The videos provided a visual world that viewers could relate to. They could watch the programmes a number of times if they wished to reinforce learning. Local scenes depicted the viewers' realities and offered culturally appropriate messages. Professor Roy McConkey helped significantly with scripting programmes, making the recordings, editing the programmes and writing the handbooks.

The videos were complimented by course books and a series of activities and exercises. These packages have now been purchased by programmes in 44 other countries and translated into Spanish, Portuguese, Italian, Farsi and Arabic.

THE APPOINTMENT OF REGIONAL COORDINATORS

Geraldine Maison-Halls and I were the National Coordinators. At first we undertook much of the training of the volunteers but, perhaps more importantly, we spent several hours each week 'accompanying' the volunteers, seeing, first-hand, the challenges they faced with the families and thereby tailoring the training to respond to these challenges. As the programme developed, the need for additional personnel to support the volunteers became urgent. Additional funding enabled the recruitment of 12 Regional Coordinators who were paid, part time, workers. They came from a variety of backgrounds including health, education, social work and parents of children with disabilities. They offered support to the volunteers as they worked with the families. Of the 12 Regional Coordinators, seven had been volunteers themselves on the programme.

The National and Regional Coordinators also played a key role in consulting with community leaders, health workers and teachers to develop a sense of ownership for the innovation within the community.

REGIONAL CBR COMMITTEES

In five regions of the country a Regional CBR Committee was elected by those involved in the local programmes. The Regional Committee managed the programme, organised training courses, social events, fund raising and opened local resource centres where families came together.

A National CBR Committee was then formed out of these Regional Committees and gradually took on more and more of the management of the programme in order to promote community ownership and do ourselves as national co-ordinators out of a job.

INCOME GENERATION

We began the CBR programme in Guyana by working with children and youth. But as they grew older the needs changed and the focus moved to need for economic independence. Our funders, AIFO, made funds available to begin a wide range of income generation projects with persons with disabilities. A total of 36 income generation programmes were funded in areas such as poultry rearing, boat making, toy making, cake decoration and hairdressing.

TRAINING FOR TEACHERS ON INCLUSIVE EDUCATION

In the interior region of the Rupununi on the border of Brazil all the teachers attended a one-week workshop on Inclusive Education that was based on the UNESCO materials, 'Schools for All' UNESCO (1988). These workshops then expanded to the coastal areas of Guyana resulting in more than 400 teachers attending the course on Inclusive Education. This training led directly to 47 children with disabilities being integrated into local schools for the first time in their lives. The training was provided by the National CBR Coordinators along with experts from the Ministry of Education. The training was also facilitated by a video training course that was created by our CBR programme for this purpose, called 'Schools for All'.

WHAT WAS THE IMPACT OF HOPEFUL STEPS?

Over a period of fifteen years, more than 420 persons were trained as facilitators, who in turn worked with more than 1,000 children, youth and adults with disabilities across Guyana. Family members met weekly at community-run, local Resource Centres that offered a range of activities such as educational activities and income generation opportunities. An emerging Disabled Persons' Organisation offered an empowering role for persons with disabilities.

The 'Hopeful Steps' CBR programme formed the basis of my PhD programme at the Institute of Education, University of London and the interested reader is referred to that research to see the empirical evidence for the value of the programme (O'Toole,B 1989) 'An evaluation of the Guyana CBR Programme, PhD Institute of Education, University of London. This research outlines the gains made by the children using both the Griffiths Test and the Portage Checklist.

However, we cannot just judge the effectiveness of the intervention in terms of gains on standardised tests or developmental checklists alone. We need to understand what the programme means to the participants.

INVOLVEMENT OF FAMILY MEMBERS

Miles and Pierre (1994) undertook an independent evaluation of the programme. They noted how parents spoke about the emotional and psychological support they had received from the volunteers. The value of CBR may lie as much in the relationship with the service agents and family members as in the specifics of the intervention they propose. Parents report feeling more relaxed, less depressed, more confident and more aware of the child's potential. Goals become more long term and realistic and hopes change from "wanting the child to be normal" to seeking help in specific areas. Parents' confidence increased. One parent commented: "Before I only looked at what my child could not do … now I look at what he can do."   Another parent, of a young lady with cerebral palsy, freely admitted, "Before, every time she was sick I actually hoped she would pass away, now I am proud of what she has achieved."

Miles and Pierre (1994) reported that children were happier, better behaved, more motivated. Parents had a keener perception of the child's progress and there were improved relationships with others in the home. Parents felt more relaxed, prouder of their children. One father commented, "This programme has united the whole family."

MOBILISING COMMUNITY RESOURCES

Volunteers increased their own self-confidence, self-respect and sense of value to others. If these volunteers are taught a range of skills, challenged to think, to take initiative; they can become agents for change, awakening their fellow villagers to their human potential and ultimately their human rights. This new model of manpower therefore has far reaching implications. The training was validated by the Institute of Adult and Continuing Education of the University of Guyana by which all the volunteers were awarded a University Certificate for participating in the programme. The tutors were trained in how to use the training packages – they would practice with their peers and get their feedback before working in the community. New tutors were paired with more experienced ones. There was also ongoing support by project personnel. It was understood that interpersonal and social skills and capacity building within the community cannot be taught by packages alone but via mentoring, accompaniment and on-going support.

COMMUNITY OWNERSHIP

An effective innovation needs a well informed and well-prepared community. Time needs to be invested in nurturing community awareness. Before commencing the programme in a new locality, we sat with the professionals in the region, service groups, Ministry personnel, and community leaders to present the programme objectives and foster local participatory involvement.

Extensive media coverage enhanced the status of the project and gave the participants the feeling that they were part of something important. As we entered new regions, the programme was announced In schools, clinics, places of worship and posters were displayed in hundreds of shops.

The elections to CBR Committees were vital in nurturing community ownership and lead to the establishment of community-run Resource Centres which were funded, in part, by government.

LESSONS LEARNT

BUILD A SOUND FOUNDATION

Careful attention was given to establish a sound foundation. The intervention was not presented as a panacea; unlike the way in which WHO promoted CBR for more than two decades with an almost evangelical, crusading zeal. The Hopeful Steps programme, by comparison, was presented as genuinely questioning the value of the approach and adapting the programme to the learning we acquired as we went along. Moreover, the Guyana CBR programme was based on a number of key factors, including; clear commitment by coordinators, high motivation of well-trained volunteers, adequate financial support, extensive media coverage, and the support of influential rehabilitation therapists.

The Guyana programme was deliberately introduced on a small scale despite invitations from several quarters to expand quickly regionally. By being small scale, it allowed quick and effective communication, coordination and decision making. But above all, we aimed to listen to persons, to meet families, persons with disabilities and the wider community and try and see the world from their point of view.

TRAINED FACILITATORS

As the programme grew in scale, the need for skilled facilitators became clear. Those managing CBR programmes need more than technical competence in disabling conditions. They need to be versed in attitude change, and how to motivate and expand the vision of others. They should be familiar with local culture. Good communication skills and the ability to form rapport with trainers, volunteers and families, is required. They need to be highly motivated and able to inspire others and possess a clear vision and know how to achieve that vision. Also, throughout their essential role is the sustaining of the community ownership of the programme.

The main role for the coordinators is that of a facilitator of human relationships. Their task is to help persons understand their own problems and then assist them in developing creative responses to those problems. Coordinators need to know when to stand back and allow participants to take the project in the most meaningful direction for them. Only then can a CBR programme develop into a community programme as opposed to a programme piloted by an outside force.

Participation cannot be brought about by political decree from the top. Persons will become involved only if they feel genuinely consulted about their needs. The goal of development becomes to influence people and not simply modify structures. Training needs to emphasise methods of facilitating consultation, developing management skills and becoming a sensitive listener. We need to focus services around the needs of people and their families. It becomes a bottom up rather than a top down model. As such, it offers more hope that it will be sustainable.

EFFECTIVENESS OF ORDINARY PEOPLE

Ordinary people – both volunteers and family members - can reduce the handicapping effects of a disability once given the appropriate knowledge and skills. Volunteers from the community feel empowered by the problem-solving roles they are asked to play. They have proven to be effective in providing emotional and practical support to families via regular home visits. They became advocates for families in dealing with others in the community and were successful builders of a network of community connections that lead to major improvements in the quality of life for families with children with disabilities.

Locally based training programmes attuned to the needs of their community were provided to the volunteers who in turn were encouraged to share their learning with families through home visits. Throughout the volunteers were 'accompanied' rather than 'supervised' by the trainers. Rather the role of the trainers is to be supportive, offering suggestions and guidance as necessary and not taking over the work with the family. The same ethos applies to volunteers in contact with families. The goal is to empower local people to solve their own problems; equip them with knowledge and skills to do so thereby helping them to realise they have within themselves the capacity to meet many of their needs.

OVERCOME NEGATIVE ATTITUDES

The problems of stigma and prejudice surrounding disability are pervasive throughout the world. However, CBR suggests that negative attitudes can be changed through local community initiatives. In every community, there were people who were well disposed to helping people with disabilities; who willingly took up the training opportunities offered by the programme and who challenged the stigma around disability as they volunteered their support to local families.

Also, many of the social and emotional needs of parents were met through building informal relationships with other parents of children with disabilities, where the script for the partnership evolves from the parents themselves. Few of the parents in the Guyana CBR programme had met other parents before the programme began. Within a year or so the majority of them had met other parents and found the meeting very helpful in realising they were not alone. There is a need for a local network of families who can provide mutual support to one another. Such a network could provide a formidable force in working for change in developing countries.

NEED FOR INTEGRATED DEVELOPMENT

Services for persons with disabilities need to be integrated into community development initiatives especially those aimed at poverty alleviation. Disability and poverty are so often synonymous. We need to move away from charity and examine the viability of income generation projects with revolving loan funds that foster self-esteem and forge relationships with others. Community perceptions change once they see persons with disabilities doing productive and valued work that makes them economically independent and of service to their communities.

Therefore, we need to question the wisdom of primarily locating CBR programmes within health structures staffed by rehabilitation workers with very limited training and expertise in development work. Chapter 3 in the present volume tries to describe the innovations in an interior area of Guyana is relevant here and demonstrates how integrated developments are possible within identified communities.

CHALLENGES FACING CBR

For all its successes, the Guyana CBR programme had its challenges some of which were resolved through time and effort but others remain because the very nature of CBR conflicts with existing service delivery. As mentioned earlier, WHO (Helander et al 1989) oversold the value of CBR is presenting it as a panacea – as relevant to children with learning difficulties, Autism or deafness. The reality may be very different. Our CBR programme responded to children, and later, adults with a very broad range of special needs. It included persons with physical, sensory and learning difficulties and ranged from children with impairments to others with profound disabilities. However, for children who are deaf, for example, a more specialised intervention is surely required that responds to their particular needs. Also another special need, that of the gifted learner, was not addressed by this intervention but is just as urgent a need.

COMMUNITY INVOLVEMENT: CATCHWORD OR REALITY?

It is clearly very challenging to mobilise previously uninvolved populations with no tradition of community participation and no mechanism for action. We soon learnt that communities are not harmonised entities; more often they are beset by petty jealousies, misuse of funds, gossip and rumour. In reality, communities are stratified. Community involvement is a new catchword. However, what channel does the community have to express itself? How can the community become involved? Coordinators are often high in technical skills but inexperienced in terms of social, political and organisational skills. Facilitating community involvement is a skill that coordinators need to develop and yet there are few training opportunities available to them. It is not surprising then that few CBR projects have moved beyond small-scale localised projects.

RELIANCE ON VOLUNTEERS

Impoverished communities may lack the human resources needed for CBR to function. There were family members whose lives were so difficult and their daily concerns too many to get deeply involved in the project. Likewise, other community members may be unwilling or unavailable to be trained. In such circumstances, a paid workforce will be needed and, in many countries, has proved successful. Our experience in Guyana was mixed. In Guyana children attend the government-run nursery schools in the mornings leaving their teachers 'free' in the afternoons for staff development and training. The Ministry of Education in one coastal area allowed 30 teachers to be trained as part of the CBR programme. However, they were far less committed to supporting the families than were the volunteers. By contrast in one of the interior regions, community health workers and teachers formed a key part of the CBR workforce. Hence redeploying existing personnel into CBR programmes needs to be done cautiously. Retraining, mentoring and supervision are essential but, even then, their personal commitment to community building is likely to be their most critical attribute.

NEW ROLE FOR REHABILITATION THERAPISTS

The key to improved services for persons with disabilities is a more innovative approach to the training of health personnel such as therapists. Their skills are essential for persons with more serious disabilities who require specialist treatments. But in order to reach many more persons when professional resources are scarce, rehabilitation therapists also need to be promoters of community development, facilitators of change and motivators of others. Their role is to mobilise resources from the community and learn how to "give away" skills. The task now becomes one of advising and inspiring rather than making unilateral decisions about specific treatments. However, changing long-established training courses and career-structures is not easy unless the political will and funding is available to bring about change.

INTEGRATING SERVICE SYSTEMS

Whilst disability is rarely a government priority, legislation is essential to protect persons with disability. The UN Convention on the Rights of Persons with Disability is a major step forward in this respect. However, ensuring these rights are upheld is a major challenge to governments internationally. Does it fall to one Ministry or is it an Inter-Ministry responsibility? How can CBR be incorporated into an existing government infrastructure to allow its expansion nationally?

But arguably the biggest conundrum is how can community ownership be maintained in government-led initiatives? We need to achieve a balance between carefully managed systems and maintaining a flexible, open-ended approach. The CBR programme challenged volunteers to be imaginative and to not simply follow a script. They were active planners and not passive functionaries. Volunteers met every ten weeks to reflect on the programme, their ideas were listened to, respected and adopted. Some of the most creative ideas for the project came out of these sessions. Internationally we need more innovative approaches to the provision of health, education, social and economic supports to persons with disabilities and to do this in ways that promote a flexible, person-centered approach.

RELIANCE ON INTERNATIONAL DONORS

In many poorer countries, CBR has developed through donor funding either to national governments or more often to NGOs as happened in Guyana. The benefits are often quickly realised but over time, possible dangers become more apparent. The programme may contract and even collapse when the donor funding ceases. From the outset, joint funding with governments is preferable; albeit on an increasing basis over a period of years. The second danger is more invidious, in that the nature of the programme is attuned more to the agenda and wishes of the donor than to the needs of the community. Ongoing, respectful dialogue between donors and recipients may help to mitigate this risk.

Ultimately though, governments must shoulder the bulk of the responsibility for the good of all their citizens. Advocacy by and for people with disabilities and their family carers is essential in ensuring this happens but so too is demonstrating the benefits that accrue from the provision of local services that strengthen communities. Economic arguments are as potent in the affluent north as in the poorer south. CBR demonstrates what can be achieved at relatively low cost for persons with disabilities. In reflection however we could and should have done more to consult with government on ways that they could incorporate the lessons learnt from this intervention into government structures. The reality however is that there was, and probably still is, little appetite on the part of decisions makers for such a role.

CONCLUSION

Few CBR programmes internationally have progressed beyond small-scale projects to the level of national programmes. Indeed, that may never happen and it may not even be desirable. In essence CBR is about human development and relationship building. It offers a far richer role to persons with disabilities and gives parents a sense that they can play a significant role in the development process. Community members become more aware of persons with disabilities in their midst, and, at times, they have played a major role in planning ways to meet their needs.

CBR offers a new style of service to rehabilitation professionals, policy makers, planners and community leaders built around human qualities rather than structures and systems. It is not surprising then that implementing this new way of working has been slow and uneven as it depends so much on the availability of persons with vision and courage who are sadly lacking in all countries. Yet until we commit to exploring new paths, there is a real danger that more conferences will be held, more declarations written, and still 98% of persons with disabilities will be blissfully unaware of the international concern being voiced on their behalf and mothers of children like Nalini will continue to keep their child with a special need hidden away.

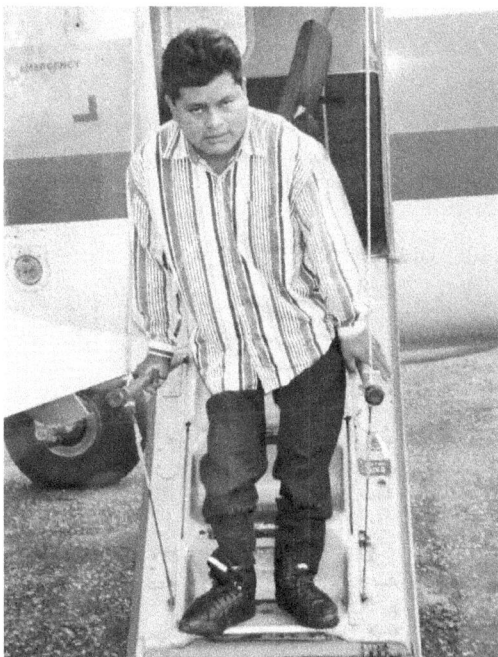

Working with persons with disability in the Rupununi

REFLECTION *by Juliet Solomon*

"Rupununi my dear, dear home, the place where I was born".
I like to think of Rupununi as the place where I was reborn and
the place that became my home.

The two VSOs, Carin Van Eldijk and Modeste Janssen had left Holland and I had left behind my four children and my mom in Trinidad to join and become a part of this "movement". I was introduced to the programme at a gathering of 99 teachers, 36 health workers and 40 village leaders for the annual two-day CBR conference held in Lethem, the administrative centre of the Rupununi. Included at this impressive function were the heads of the region's administrative offices and the Director and staff of the programme from Georgetown. The talent and giftedness of the programme and its peoples shone brilliantly as I stood in awe and wondered about what I was getting myself into.

The CBR programme sought to introduce awareness of children with disabilities, early stimulation for preschool children and literacy training for teachers. The hallmark of the programme was its holistic approach to problem-solving which called for a leadership that included the heads within the community, ie the Toshao or village leader, the headteacher and the health worker. Another tenet of the programme was the stipulation that the CBR programme had to work within the given infrastructure. I thought this was so appropriate as it called for harmony and inclusion. I was introduced to the heads of the various government offices with whom I would have to work when planning and executing workshops.

As I began to understand the programme and the impact it was having on the region I became deeply moved by the people who were actually responsible for this impact. The health workers carried out their work to the very best of their abilities and with more challenges than one cared to tell of.

The teachers were hungry to learn and during that period there were very few who had been officially trained. The CBR programme conducted Literacy training for all 100% of the teachers and soon there were enough skilled teachers who then joined the team of trainers and themselves conducted training in smaller groups within their communities and in other regions.

I used the word "movement" earlier on because the programme did take the region by storm. There was training every single weekend, sometimes starting from the Friday, for every month of the year. The principal trainers, though respected, embraced the skills and knowledge of those being trained and used every opportunity to encourage growth and further enhancement of these skills. Participants felt validated and empowered, another key for success.

The CBR programme had as one of its strengths a spirit of inclusion. The late evening programme brought everyone out, swelling the school buildings into the yards. Highlighted at these gatherings was raw talent in the performing arts that was funny and stimulating. The skits and songs reflected the theme and essence of the training topics. This was also an opportunity for non-workshop participants to join in the fun and demonstrate their talent through song, story-telling or giving a joke.

But how were these three-member teams to return to their villages and teach their fellow villagers? They were sent home with a tool kit, much of which they themselves had made during the workshops and some basic materials and stationery. They held regular CBR village meetings. At these meetings they shared and then organized their own training and reported back at sub-regional meetings. Their pride in what they had accomplished was evident in their sharing.

The Early Stimulation module gave birth to the video package "Where There is no Nursery". This resulted in a cross-sectoral innovation in which health workers, teachers and community leaders started having training sessions with parents to spread their knowledge on parents being the best first-trainers/teachers. Mothers in particular then took it upon themselves to start a movement on their own and joined forces to teach their children. This in turn gave birth to nursery schools being built with funding from UNICEF. The nursery school in Potarinau Village is one such success story. The parents were the teachers here and when the UNICEF staff visited, these parents moved to the forefront and showed off their skills, humbly yet brilliantly!

These early successes around pre-school learning were instrumental in helping the government to prioritise pre-school education in this remote region, with specific targeted investments in construction of nursery schools in several other areas of the Rupununi and the training and appointment of nursery school teachers.

Income generation was another area in which CBR became involved. In the village of Nappi one family engaged in pig rearing, a mother of a child with cerebral palsy engaged in poultry farming and another family focussed on peanut production.

Because of this multi-sector approach and integrated teaching and learning processes, community development soon became stronger. Clearly there were many challenges due to the remoteness of the region, frequent flooding only to be followed by droughts.

The CBR programme was based on harmony and togetherness. The fact that such large groups could be organized and work successfully to produce successful outcomes is a testimony to our true desire for peace and harmony, for laughter and for love, for equality and development.

REFLECTION *by*
Emeritus Professor Roy McConkey

Community-Based Rehabilitation in Guyana:
Back to the Future

The CBR programme in Guyana was a decade and more ahead of its time. The novel concepts it pioneered are now widely accepted as the bedrock for services to people with disabilities world-wide. 'Hopeful Steps' was built around three basic assumptions that thirty years ago would have been thought fanciful, if not down-right dangerous.

First, disability is a social issue not a medical condition. Admittedly physical, sensorial and mental impairments can be remedied and ameliorated with the help of doctors and therapists but often it is the social consequences of the impairments that are much more disabling. The stigma, the social isolation, the poverty, the lack of educational and employment opportunities all compound and magnify the impact of any bodily imperfection. Hence the modern recognition that disability requires a societal and not just a clinical response. The UN Convention on the Rights of Persons with Disabilities (2006) states this in its preamble:

"Persons with disabilities include those who have long-term physical, mental, intellectual or sensory impairments which in interaction with various barriers may hinder their full and effective participation in society on an equal basis with others".

Creating the conditions for the 'full and effective participation' of children, teenagers and adults with disabilities in their families and in their local communities was the prime purpose of Hopeful Steps. Their innovative strategy was a gamble that many disability experts of yesteryear would have thought was doomed to fail. But they showed that training and supporting communities was not only feasible but it yielded a much better quality of life for many more persons and their families, and at a fraction of the cost than clinic-based rehabilitation services.

Secondly, Guyana put the community into CBR. When WHO launched CBR in the early 1980s, the focus was on rehabilitation in the community. It heralded more a change in location rather than ethos. But the programme in Guyana emphasised community not rehabilitation. Indeed in my first encounter with it, I was puzzled as to why the co-ordinators had not set up a database of all the disabled children and families they had enrolled on 'their programme'. How blinded was I by old notions! But as their programmes evolved, it became apparent that community development required a much broader focus than training volunteers to be home visitors. So management committees were formed, educational resource centres opened, income generation schemes commenced and advocacy organisations started. Thirty years on, WHO relaunched CBR as a matrix of five key components – health, education, livelihood, social and empowerment. Imitation, they say, is the sincerest form of flattery.

Thirdly, relationships are more powerful than systems. Brian has emphasised the centrality of relationship building within the Guyanese programme and the amount of time and effort they invested in listening to the needs of people with disabilities and in responding to the reality of community life in towns and villages throughout the country. Unlike other development initiatives, they did not come with their own ready-made solutions but rather choose to accompany, guide and at times cajole people to find their own solutions. The building of trusted and respectful relationships is under-appreciated within current service systems. Yet for most people with disabilities, relationships add most to the quality of their lives. Today there is much greater emphasis on person-centred services and the creation of informal supports within local communities for people availing of social services because of old age, disability or mental health issues. However we still have much to learn as to how to inculcate the personal qualities *required of service personnel that are attuned to these goals. But Guyana CBR provides an excellent model of what is possible.*

Brian rightly identifies the challenges to sustaining innovative community-owned programmes for disadvantaged communities to which Guyana was not immune. The reason for failures can be readily enumerated but the solutions are harder to discern, still less to implement. But of this we can be sure. We need to break away from old ways of thinking and well-worn paths of action that have proven to be dead-ends. Rather we need visionaries who can dream of things that never were and have the dedication and determination to make them a reality. Perhaps that is the principal lesson to take from the CBR Programme in Guyana.

United Nations Convention of Rights of Persons with Disabilities (2006). Available at: http://www.un.org/disabilities/convention/conventionfull.shtml.

World Health Organization (WHO). (2010). Community-based Rehabilitation: CBR Guidelines (Geneva: WHO), Available at: www.who.int/disabilities/cbr/guidelines/en/index.html

APPENDIX #1:
VIDEO TRAINING PACKAGES DEVELOPED ON THE GUYANA CBR PROGRAMME

1. **Hopeful Steps**

    Six, 15 minute programmes which examine the following areas; learning to move, talk, think and be independent. Offers assessment and teaching ideas. Another programme focuses on how to make toys out of readily available materials. Accompanied by a 90-page illustrated teaching manual.

2. **Community Action on Disability**

    Eight, 15 minute, programmes which examine some of the key themes of CBR, including; community and parental involvement, training strategies, working with teachers, community networks and motivating volunteers. Accompanied by a 62-page illustrated manual.

3. **Identification of Disabilities**

    A 25-minute video for Primary Health Care workers and CBR volunteers offering simple ways to identify children with disabilities. Accompanied by two illustrated manuals, Identification of Disabilities and Introduction to Disabilities.

4. **Facts for Life**

    A 50-minute video which analyses the major challenges in developing healthy lives. Focuses on; breast feeding, timing of births, immunization, AIDS and malaria. Accompanied by a teacher's guide and a set of teaching brochures.

5. **A New Tomorrow**

   Eight 14 minute programmes which examine the development of children within the context of the Amerindian experience of the interior of Guyana. Offers simple assessment and teaching ideas. Accompanied by a 70 page illustrated manual. Produced in association with UNESCO.

6. **Educating communities about disability**

   Presents a number of puppet programmes designed to increase awareness in the community of the needs of persons with a disability. Accompanied by a 60-page illustrated manual on how to make puppets and write scripts.

7. **All Together**

   A series of programmes designed to offer support to regular class teachers as they integrate children with special needs into the ordinary school.

CHAPTER 2

"On the Wings of Words": Literacy as a means of Empowerment

Brian and Pamela O'Toole

INTRODUCTION

An irate parent came to see us. She complained that her 10-year-old was writing all over the walls of her unpainted house. He was writing sentences like: 'I can help you.' and 'Will you go to help?' He had written more than 50 sentences in an expression of sheer joy. What greater reward could there be for one of the literacy facilitators who had finally broken through in teaching the child how to read and write, even if it meant that the walls of the house were now rather more colourful.

Other parents reflected on the successes of the literacy training programme with comments like: "My grandson's reading report went from 45% to 98%", "…. I never knew I could teach my son how to read" and "It made me feel like I was a teacher."

Over a twenty-year, period from 1994 to 2014, the On the Wings of Words (OWOW) literacy programme was established in eight of the ten regions of Guyana. More than 4,000 volunteer literacy facilitators were trained who in turn worked with 15,000 children and youth improving their reading skills and powers of expression and comprehension.

THE SCALE OF THE CHALLENGE

For far too long Guyana had boasted very unrealistic figures concerning the literacy standards in the country. In 1998 the UN were quoting a literacy rate of 98.1% in Guyana (UN Development Report, 1998). By sharp contrast, a study in 1994 by Professor Jennings, from the University of Guyana, demonstrated clearly that 89% of out-of-school youth were functionally illiterate. They were unable to read even a simple sentence. (Jennings, 1994)

There followed, in 2000, an extensive survey of 5,000 twelve-year olds in 22 schools throughout the country, conducted by the Varqa Foundation (VF) on behalf of British Department for International Development that administers Overseas Aid. This revealed that more than 20% of the sample could not read a single word and this despite the fact they had spent more than seven years at school.

Guyana, of course, is not alone in this respect. One billion persons in the world, because of their illiteracy, are deprived of health information, safety guidelines, novels, and reading newspapers, all of which are as inaccessible to them as shopping in a supermarket in China would be to us.

RETHINKING LITERACY AND EDUCATION

Arbab (1992) presents a new definition of literacy. The minimum requirements of education need to be conceived in terms of the basic knowledge, qualities, skills, attitudes and capacities that enable individuals to become conscious subjects of their own growth, and active, responsible participants in a systematic process of building a new world order.

As the Bahá'í International Task Force for Literacy (1989) observed, 'people need to become empowered as learners, to gain access to the kind of education and knowledge which will enable them both to assume control over their own processes of growth, and to become active, responsible participants in a systematic process of social change.'

One outgrowth of this international experience has been the realization of the need to appreciate the culture of the people who are to be served in any literacy programme. Another realization, voiced by Arbab (1992), is that 'literacy campaigns cannot exist outside the context of a social

On the Wings of Words training sessions

On the Wings of Words training sessions

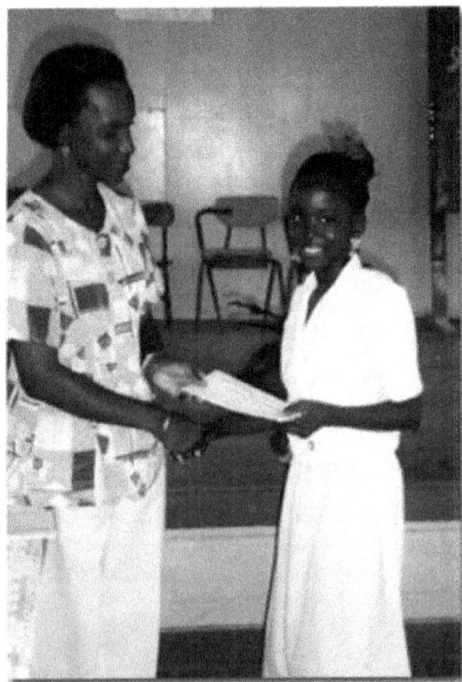

The first On the Wings of Words training session

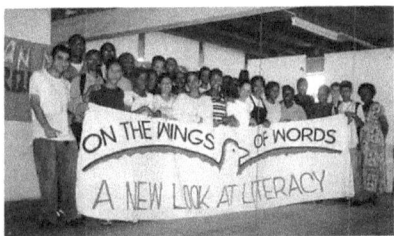

On the Wings of Words training sessions

Baha'is spreading the gift of knowledge through reading

Local program reaches out to children in Guyana

By Craig Campbell
Staff Writer

Baha'i communities in Dundas, Ancaster and Hamilton picked up 40,000 extra books from school libraries and sent them to remote villages in Guyana.

Small libraries were set up in some peculiar places — like under houses built on stilts. But there was a problem. Children were getting the books, but they were only leafing through them or looking at pictures. The children couldn't read.

Pam O'Toole, a resident of Guyana, helped organize a training session. The idea was to show adults and youth how to teach the children to read.

"Many people came. Many types of people," Ms. O'Toole said. "We didn't have enough space, material or trainers, but it was a great week."

Since 1995, three training sessions have been held every year. More than 1,700 literacy instructors have been trained and a minimum of 7,000 children have been reached. But no one knows for sure how many are being taught.

Dundas resident Pat Cameron has made three trips to Guyana to help train instructors. Her husband is a doctor who has gone on medical missions to Guyana. He

More than 1,700 literacy instructors have been trained and 7,000 children reached.

mentioned his wife was a teacher at Colin Macdonald Alternative School, and Ms. O'Toole wanted her there right away.

"I get up early, work really hard, and get to bed really late," Ms. Cameron said of her trips to Guyana.

Fellow Baha'i and Dundas resident Michael Larsh heard about the On the Wings of Words literacy program from Ms. Cameron.

As a documentary filmmaker, Mr. Larsh saw it as a chance to tell a great story.

"It's an indigenous program," he said, explaining Guyana residents are the ones who do all the teaching. "It's an example of a local community working with others to identify a problem, and going through the process to find answers."

Mr. Larsh joined Ms. Cameron and Ms. O'Toole in Guyana for one week, interviewing and filming for the half-hour documentary in April.

"The program is very self-sufficient, and is served well by the Guyanese," Ms. Cameron said. "I feel my input was marginal."

On her last visit, she showed the local volunteer instructors how to make simple "flip" books. They could be made without glue, staples or other binding.

"The children could write their own stories and put them in the book," Ms. Cameron said.

Writing their own stories inspires the children to read, write and even tell their stories to their families.

The ability to read, Bahai's believe, gives people the ability to investigate spirituality and develop values.

Exchange of ideas

"There's an exchange of ideas, reflection on spiritual perspective, control and action," Ms. Cameron said. "These are the things that are done in addition to the mechanics (of reading)."

But because the program is an indigenous one, Mr. Larsh pointed out the majority of the instructors and children are not followers of the Baha'i faith.

"The program is for the community," he said.

After their training sessions, the instructors head back to their own communities, which are sometimes very small and isolated.

They work with their neighbourhood's children wherever possible — on their own verandah, someone's living room or maybe under one of the homes built on stilts.

"The model is being used in other developing countries," Mr. Larsh said. "It's more applicable to them. They have more in common."

While he was in Guyana filming the documentary, he saw a school teacher approach one of the program's volunteer learning instructors.

The teacher was very impressed with how far one particular student had advanced in reading.

"What miracle have you done?" the teacher asked.

Mr. Larsh's On the Wings of Words documentary was on Vision TV on Dec. 6 at 10:30 p.m., and will be re-broadcast at a later date.

Dundas Star News • Wednesday, December 20, 2000•

Photo by Craig Campbell

MICHAEL LARSH, Pam O'Toole and Pat Cameron screen Mr. Larsh's documentary about the On the Wings of Words literacy program.

'On the Wings of Wo

GEORGETOWN – A growing need among the young and old to learn how to read or better improve this essential survival skill has increased the demand for a handful of successful local literacy programmes like 'On The Wings Of Words'.

Organisers hope this reading programme started in 1996 will help 'shape' young Guyanese, the "citizens of tomorrow" with literacy skills and a very strong spiritual basis not dogmatic in any one religion.

Youths discuss different spiritual themes and memorise short quotations helping them to reflect on moral and spiritual concepts, which act as guiding principles for living and provide the young with a greater understanding of themselves in society.

Reading manuals prepared mostly by teachers at School of the Nations in Parade Street, Kingston had initially targeted ages four to 16 but even adults can now benefit from them.

At the last reading sessions held June 3 to 6, 2002 there were at least 300 participants – teachers, parents and volunteers wanting to be taught pre-literacy and literacy skills to teach children how to read or improve their reading. Since this literacy-training programme began more than 3000 facilitators from all across Guyana have been trained, and more than 10,000 youngsters have benefited.

'On The Wings Of Words' programme publishes its own manuals, readers, workbooks and newsletters. Reading classes are organised every three months. All classes are free and anybody wanting to learn how to improve reading skills is invited to attend these sessions.

The upcoming training session would be held from October 7 to 9 from 16:30 hrs to 18:00hrs at School of the Nations. It is anticipated that, apart from the new attendees, many of the persons who participated in previous reading sessions will return to do the next level, says Pamela O'Toole, Principal, Secondary Department, at School of the Nations.

'On The Wings Of Words' reading programme is not only accessible in Georgetown.

In outlying areas like Parika, Berbice or Linden, sessions are kept at schools

By Sharon

or community centers.

Every three months persons are taught one reading level and are given a 'reader', cardboard and colour markers to make the games that help make reading fun for children, said O'Toole.

Once the trainers of the programme are working with very large groups of people the participants have to purchase a workbook that cost $200. Persons who are taught the reading skills are expected to practice at home what they've learnt and return in another three months' time to learn new skills in another level of reading.

For older students, this reading programme offers three reading levels while 'nursery' students need to complete six levels of reading skills. O'Toole said there are 'dropouts' after the first level of training but she knows that at least 30 per cent of the persons who come seeking skills to read do return to complete the other levels of reading.

Parents, especially, have been very dedicated to finishing the programme because after practicing with

rds' boosting literacy

Natasha Lall

their children the skills they had been taught there were improvements in the levels of reading among children, said O'Toole.

The programme also attracts teachers from various primary schools who want to learn how to help students at school progress in reading. There have been subsequent feedbacks from parents who claimed that reading has helped their children move from 20 per cent to 80 per cent on their school's academic report card.

"Those people who have continued with the programme regularly have had profound progress," says O'Toole, adding, "I think the (reading) materials really work." Penny Gaime, Deputy Principal of the Nursery division at School of the Nations said people living outside Georgetown are made aware of the reading programme via advertisements in the print or electronic media, or even the Regional Education Officer who would inform schools about the sessions.

In some areas, organisers inform various contact persons who may have previously been trained at some of the reading classes, to help organise the sessions.

O'Toole says 'On The Wings Of Words' reading programme has covered nine of Guyana's ten administrative regions. The need for literacy programmes is spread across the country and there is no single region that is worse off in reading than another, according to Gaime.

No real reason has yet been found to explain levels of illiteracy among persons who had been exposed to schooling at one point or another. O'Toole suggested that in some cases it might be a "gender issue" where girls are often times kept at home and not encouraged to go to school. Interestingly, at least 98 per cent of all the participants of 'On The Wings Of Words' reading programme are women.

The programme was formulated to target ages 4 to 16 but in recent times adults with poor reading skills have been attending the reading sessions hoping to develop their own reading skills, said Gaime. Gaime teaches parents of children in the nursery and she has been observing that some of the adults in her class have been attending simply to, themselves, grasp elementary skills like phonics or matching games needed to learn how to read.

Gaime said, however, that 'On The Wings Of Words' reading books are also designed to help even adults who want to learn how to read, or improve their reading.

Given the desire of adults to learn how to read - 'On The Wings Of Words' reading programme may in future make provisions for school drop outs or adults who may not know how to read well.

It is likely these persons will have to pay for this type of training that should initially be done in Georgetown, said O'Toole.

While Varqa Foundation generally sponsors 'On The Wings Of Words' reading programmes, the funding

comes from the Baha'i international community, the Guyana Book Foundation, the Gender Equity Programme of the Canadian International Development Agency (CIDA), the British High Commission and UNICEF.

Varqa is an independent Non-Governmental Organisation (NGO) based in Guyana. The Board of Varqa Foundation have been inspired by their conviction that the principles, concepts and counsels contained in the writings of the Baha'i provides humanity with an invaluable source of wisdom and inspiration in its search for a new path of development.

The Varqa Foundation's primary area of expertise is communication, education and training in various development sectors.

Specifically, Varqa staffers have experience in education – formal and non-formal, health, gender and development, project management and professional effectiveness. This NGO has associates in Canada, United States and the United Kingdom.

The materials inside 'On The Wings Of Words' reading books are compiled by teachers from School of the Nations, who assess what works best among children and older age groups.

During training the participants will learn different methods in the teaching of reading, the role of games, songs and drama in reinforcing skills learnt, the making of teaching aids and games, and how to use the manuals, reading books and workbooks effectively.

ideology', especially as expressed in the vision of what a society is and how it should be transformed. 'Literacy therefore includes, but goes far beyond, the basic skills of reading and writing'.

The International Task Force for Literacy (1989) noted that conditions of mass poverty and illiteracy render people more vulnerable to the forces of terrorism, ethnic violence and other forms of social disruption. Literacy efforts can offer constructive means for maximizing social stability and economic benefit for all. Implicit in this understanding was the idea that development meant becoming like the industrialized nations of the West. A number of features of life in the unindustrialized countries were regarded as synonymous with obstacles to development. Examples of this were the extended family, respect for elders and authorities, religious beliefs and attachment to community tradition.

Economic growth was taken as the simple indicator of development. Economic growth meant that people would produce more and consume more. Such a condition necessitated a labour force that was far more productive than traditional societies seemed to generate. Such an improved labour force had to be literate in order to read manuals, understand instructions and participate in production processes that were different from what the workers had been accustomed to. Functional literacy therefore meant literacy in the area of productivity and consumption.

A basic assumption in this view of literacy was that the essential motivating force for adults to participate in literacy programmes was the attraction that they would be able to earn more and consume more and in the process, move up the social ladder. The goal of most functional literacy programmes has been to develop the economic potential of the individual, thereby contributing to the 'human capital' of the developing country. To assess the effectiveness of early functional literacy programmes, questions often centered on increased savings and spending power, reduced family size and the breaking away from traditional activities of the community.

A major limitation of early approaches to the teaching of literacy was the way in which the learner remained a passive recipient of information. Functional literacy did not change the behaviour and attitudes of the learners. Its role was simply transferring knowledge from the 'teacher' to the 'learner' without transforming him or her.

EDUCATION FOR LIBERATION

Paulo Freire formulated his views on education and literacy in the early 1960s in Brazil. Freire's analysis interpreted the situation of the illiterate masses in terms of dependence and oppression. A careful analysis of the teacher-student relationship revealed the teacher acting as a narrator and the students becoming passive receptacles for the teacher to fill. In the process of narrating, the concepts became removed from reality, lifeless, static and compartmentalized. Instead of communicating, the teacher deposited education and the students merely received, memorized and repeated. A good teacher poured information into empty vessels and good students were identified as those who allowed themselves to be filled up. Education was not seen as a process of enquiry, but as a process of receiving, cataloguing and storing the deposits to be returned on request.

Freire (1972) called this the 'banking concept' of education, consequences of which are
- the conquest of the learners;
- the division of the learners;
- the manipulation of the learners;
- the invasion of the culture of the learners.

REDEFINING EDUCATION

Although the rate of illiteracy continues to fall, the absolute number of people who cannot read is rising. A fundamental international educational crisis looms before us, with schools on the one hand inadequately meeting the needs of their populations, and on the other vast numbers of children deprived of any education.

The requirements of justice state that literacy is a basic human right. To combat this crisis, not only will international cooperation and political will need to be profoundly reassessed, but a new concept of education will need to be defined that enables students to participate in their own growth and work towards the betterment of both themselves and the societies in which they live.

In an attempt to articulate a new concept of what education can achieve, the Bahá'í International Community identifies the goal of education as transformation of individuals and society in the process of creating a new world order based on moral values and spiritual individuals. The task of education is to develop the latent capacities in human nature through a desire to serve others, exercising the will to effect personal and social change, and the realization that the pursuit of wealth is not the key to human happiness and self-respect, but involvement in noble purposes for the advancement of mankind.

Literacy is therefore far more than the acquisition of the mechanical skills of reading and writing. We need to explore ways to develop the creativity of expression, the ability to use the power of the word, to read with good comprehension, develop critical thinking and to express ideas with clarity.

EVOLUTION OF THE "ON THE WINGS OF WORDS" (OWOW) LITERACY PROGRAMME

The OWOW literacy programme grew out of the community programmes described in other chapters in this book; on Community Based Rehabilitation (CBR) and the Youth Can Move the World (YCMTW) programmes. The OWOW programme was initially carried out in 1994 within the Bahá'í community but by 1996 the training was offered to the wider Guyanese public.

In our early visits to the Rupununi region, I took part in a Conference that had been organized for all the Head Teachers of the region. They said that their most pressing need was training in literacy. In travelling throughout the Rupununi region for the Guyana CBR programme and the Bahá'í Community Health Partnership we heard constantly about the need to teach children and youth of the region how to read.

In 1994, Varqa Foundation arranged with a Bahá'í community in Canada to ship 40,000 books to Guyana. These books then formed libraries in 60 coastal and 40 interior villages. The Canadian Organisation for Development through Education (CODE) then challenged Varqa to produce a Children's Newspaper. VF produced 15,000 copies of this newspaper each month for two years. However, it soon became obvious that despite the fact that the villages now had a library for the first time and access to a children's newspaper, many of the children and youth simply could not read the books or access the information in the newspaper. Training was urgently needed therefore for the villagers to make effective use of their new libraries and reading materials.

Learning to read is a rocky path on which so many fall and, failing to regain their balance, make very little progress. Like a scattered jigsaw, the fragments of their reading skills lie unrelated and isolated in their minds; rendering it impossible to make any sense of the written word. The OWOW programme endeavoured to give persons a glimpse of the jigsaw picture and help them piece the puzzle together. Its goal was to promote reading and comprehension skills and empower children and youth to take control of their own lives via fostering moral and spiritual consequences, critical reading skills, improved consultation and decision-making skills and increased self-confidence.

A Literacy Task Force was formed with the involvement of the Baha'is. One of the first actions of this Task Force was to undertake an intensive two-day study of the available guidance on the promotion of literacy and to try to understand the reasons for the failure of so many innovations in the teaching of reading that had been attempted around the world. Armed with these insights the OWOW programme began to emerge in 1996. It was concluded that literacy is more than the acquisition of the mechanical skills of reading and writing and acknowledged the need to explore ways to develop the creativity of expression, the ability to use the power of the word, to read with good comprehension and to express ideas with clarity.

OWOW uses the analogy of a bird taking flight. One wing is the physical aspect of humankind, the other is the spiritual. Traditional education only acknowledges one wing, the physical side of the child. As a result, the other wing has largely withered. It is only when both wings are developed that the bird can soar. OWOW has attempted to strengthen both wings. Hence in addition to focusing on the mechanics of reading, the OWOW programme examined the Power of the Holy Word, the Nobility of Man, the importance of spiritual education for children, caring discipline, truthfulness, and the love and fear of God.

TRAINING FACILITATORS

The OWOW programme was born in early 1996 in the wider Guyanese community and in July of that year more than 200 persons, from a wide range of backgrounds, gathered in a school to learn about the programme. The sight at that first training, of a nun, a Rastafarian and a woman dressed in a chador, sitting side by side studying spiritual guidance from the Holy books, was an eloquent portent of things to come. There followed a five-day training that laid the foundation for a programme that, within a decade, would touch literally thousands of persons in all areas of the country.

The mornings of that first training focused not on literacy but rather on the spiritual foundation to the programme. It was realized that reading alone would not overcome the challenges of abuse, poverty, war and injustice. The three fundamental themes of the OWOW programme were therefore outlined:

- Man is a noble being
- How do we know what is right or wrong?
- How can we ensure we do what is right?

The afternoons were devoted to the other wing of the OWOW approach; the mechanics of reading adopting both the 'Look and Say' approach and phonics. This was carried out along with the promotion of games, songs, skits and the gathering of baseline data. From the outset those participating were strongly discouraged from seeking any payment for the classes as facilitators.

For the remedial reader, there are three Levels of materials with each level being comprised of a Reading Book and a Student Workbook to practice the new Look and Say words and the phonics rules. A Facilitator's Manual guided the volunteer through every step of the two components of the programme – the Spiritual and the Practical.

SPIRITUAL COMPONENT

The Spiritual component studied themes and virtues including Good Deeds, Following the Spiritual Path, Honesty, Purity, Love and Generosity. The structure of a typical Lesson in the Facilitator's Manual comprised of two short quotations from the major religions on the virtue one of which was to be memorized, questions to assist with comprehension of the quotations and to understand what the virtues "look like in actions", with games to play and a song to learn. The lesson culminated with a story related to the virtue.

For example, in the two lessons on Love the following quotations are used for discussion and memorization;

"You shall love your neighbor as yourself" (Christianity);

"Not one of you is a believer until he loves for his brother what he loves for himself." (Islam);

"In the garden of thy heart plant naught but the rose of love" (Bahá'í Faith);

"Only by love can men see me, and know me, and come unto me." (Hinduism).

Students select the quotation they wish to memorize. In order to understand what the virtue "looks like" the following questions were asked and discussed

Tell if each of these sentences is True or False.	
When we show love we:	
1. are patient.	2. are kind.
3. are full of envy.	4. are rude.
5. are selfish.	6. are easily angered.
7. don't forgive.	8. start arguments.
9. are thoughtful	10. hit children.

List five people who could be considered our 'neighbors' or our 'brother'.	
What would we love for ourselves?	
1. pain?	2. sorrow?
3. arguments?	4. joy?
5. peacefulness?	6. fear?
7. kindness?	8. good friends?
9. forgiveness?	10. injustice?
11. truthfulness?	12. helpfulness?

Discuss
1. Do you think weeds could grow in the garden of our heart?

For the two lessons on Love the story was of Clara Barton, the founder of the American Red Cross, highlighting her love for her brother and mankind.

In order to give time to understand each virtue, usually two lessons were devoted to each one, giving students the opportunity to share their actions during the week that demonstrated the virtue.

PRACTICAL COMPONENT

Each lesson comprises detailed guidance on how to teach the new Look and Say words and the phonics rules and sounds, games to play for practice, and answers to the pages in the Workbook. The support continues with guidance on questions to ask after each page in the Reading Book. Spelling and Grammar activities are included as well as games to practice. In this way the volunteers feel confident in their ability to systematically teach the students one small step at a time.

THE OWOW PROGRAMME IN ACTION

Publicizing the programme was done primarily through newspaper advertisements. The extremely positive response to these adverts lead to regular training programmes of up to 350 people. Subsequently newsletters were sent to each volunteer outlining upcoming trainings.

The volunteers came from all walks of life. Many were teachers keen to improve their skills in the teaching of reading, some were parents, siblings and grandparents working with their own children and grandchildren. Others were community workers, members of service organisations like Rotary and the Lions Clubs, coaches, housewives, members of church groups, social workers, concerned members of the community and young people wishing to help those younger students in need.

Facilitators worked in a wide variety of settings, in school buildings, church halls, in community centres, in people's living rooms and the "bottom house" of residencies (houses are built on stilts), even under a tree and in the park.

Some volunteers held regular sessions once or twice a week, but many recognized the value of an intensive focus on the intervention and worked four mornings a week for four to five weeks in the summer holidays. The dedication of some groups of volunteers spanned decades.

Many volunteers came to the trainings as they had already recognized and identified students in need of assistance. Others were already working with children and youth and were delighted to have a structured programme to support their efforts. For those now trained but with no immediate students identified with whom they could work, a number of ways were employed to identify students. In a number of instances volunteers sought assistance from the schools to locate students most in need. A popular way for many was to hold a community meeting in the neighbourhood; inviting persons whose children could benefit from such an intervention. Others invited the young people sitting on the street corners to join. There seemed to be no shortage of students. Indeed, one facilitator commented, "The illiterate are not falling through the cracks in the school system, they are pouring out!" In some cases, the volunteers were overwhelmed by those seeking help and had to prioritize those in greatest need. Parents were approached to pledge to send the students selected to the classes every session as they were being given a place on the programme that others dearly wanted.

Many volunteers added additional skills-training to their classes; teaching the youth income generating skills, even etiquette and good manners and building self-esteem and confidence. It was heartwarming to note that the spirit of volunteerism was maintained by many for years working selflessly with cohort after cohort of children eager to move along the path to reading fluency. These steadfast volunteers were recognized by the Literacy Task Force at graduations and award ceremonies.

Commitment to the programme was evident by the numbers of returning facilitators for further training. In the October 2007 OWOW training course for example, nine persons came back for their 2nd OWOW training, 19 for their third, 10 for the 4th and 33 for the 5th or more training. One facilitator who attended every programme was asked why she keeps returning for more training to which she replied 'On the Wings of Words is (my) 'me' programme.'

OWOW TEACHING MATERIALS:

OWOW materials were developed for two different groups - children progressing through Nursery to Grade 3 and for the older remedial reader (Levels 1 – 3). The content was the same but the method of introduction, activities and workbook format differed to suit the relevant ages. As the title of the programme indicates, reading skills were broken down using a Task Analysis approach into small steps. The rationale being that by teaching reading skills in small steps in a systematic way and laying a foundation for more complex skills, students would then progress smoothly from skill to skill.

Level 1 students are introduced to both Look and Say words and phonics skills. By initially using nine Look and Say or sight words that can be combined into over 150 different sentences (go, can, a, to, you, will, help, I, not, we) students achieve early reading success: an important factor for the remedial reader. By introducing letter sounds and blending them, the Look-and-Say words are quickly supplemented by additional words (Sam, fan, an, am, ran, ram). Skills are introduced then practiced through the medium of games, activities, the Student Workbook and the Reading Book: On the Path.

This approach differed from the methods used in the school system which lacked materials and often left the teachers to tread the path of the teaching of reading with merely lists of skills to be learned and guidelines for content. Too often in the schools, instruction was sporadic, random and resulted in reading and spelling words that were topical rather than phonetic. Parents were left to struggle to teach their First grader a list of words like apple, banana, orange, mango and guava.

The Box below lists the materials that were developed for the OWOW programme for the students in Nursery to Grade 3:

'In the Garden': (Workbook) covers the development of pre-reading skills at the nursery level focusing on: hand-eye coordination, visual discrimination, oral language, auditory discrimination and early phonic skills

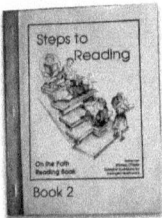

'On the Path' (Reading and Workbook) introduces nine Look and Say words and five letter sounds, blending of the 5 sounds

'Down the Road' and 'Over the Hill' (Reading and Workbooks) cover the remaining consonants and short vowel sounds, blending them into words and compound words. Look and Say words continued to be introduced

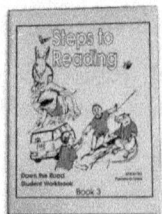

'Through the Forest' (Reading and Workbook) covers long vowel sounds

'By the Creek' (Reading and Workbook) completes the phonic rules

For the remedial reader the materials above were compiled into Levels 1 – 3. Teaching instruction, student demonstration of knowledge and skills and workbook format were the most notable differences.

Children's Newspaper: to further develop emerging reading skills

Games and Teaching aids: the games and teaching aids were constructed during the trainings for use with the students.

The materials that were developed for the Facilitators consisted of five Facilitator's Manuals offering the sections on the spiritual components, detailed lessons guides, answers to Workbook pages, questions to ask for each Reading Book page, questions to discuss, songs to teach, spelling to learn, grammar rules and games to reinforce reading materials. Additional teaching activities were also included that could be used if necessary.

Pamphlets for parents on; nursery rhymes, songs, stories, learning colours, learning to count, and the development of thinking skills

Videos: 2 x 75-minute videos focused on; early stimulation, making toys and games and pre-reading activities

Inspirational Words: from the various Holy Writings including prayers for children, guidance on the qualities of the teacher and reflections on the power of the Holy Word

Pre-tests, Post-tests and Progress Records of the students; pre-test baseline data information was gathered before the interventions commenced, Records of Attendance were maintained, notes on student level of participation, and data on the passages of Holy Writings memorized were noted. After a period of time the Post-test was administered by another volunteer to ensure impartiality and records kept of student progress.

LOOK BACK STEP AHEAD (LBSA) QUARTERLY MEETINGS

Every quarter a LBSA meeting would be organized to offer ongoing support to the volunteers, give additional instruction in teaching methods, celebrate successes and troubleshoot any issues or problems. New content focused on: story-telling, caring communication, effective discipline, story writing and book making.

The LBSA Meetings were a time when facilitators could request assistance with teaching strategies, discipline, sourcing materials etc. They were open to all the facilitators and usually well attended. Although the members of the Literacy Task Force facilitated these meetings, there was much sharing of ideas and strategies that had worked for the individual facilitators. Key parts of these meetings were fellowship and encouragement and celebration of successes.

FUNDING

Over the years OWOW has secured funding from a wide range of groups including: Guyana Book Foundation, Canadian Organisation for Development through Education (CODE), Gender Equality Fund of CIDA, UNICEF, Ministry of Education, Government of Luxembourg, Unity Foundation (Luxembourg), and the German Embassy.

The funding was utilized to advertise the trainings, print the Student Workbook and Reading Book and the Facilitator's Manuals. A copy of each was given to the volunteers. In addition, materials such as gift wrap was purchased and printed shape and letter pages made to make the picture cards, shape cards and letter cards. In order to ensure greater durability, Scotch tape was used to 'laminate' the games designed by the volunteers and the cards made during the trainings. In the interior regions money was utilized to transport participants to a central location and cover the costs of food and board.

The trainers on the programme worked long hours for small stipends to ensure the trainings were held. A full-time coordinator of the OWOW Programme was appointed to mail out the newsletters and keep in regular touch with the volunteers offering support and guidance, troubleshooting, and delivering additional books and resources when necessary. The Coordinators, over the years, played a key role in supporting and accompanying the facilitators, travelling extensively throughout the country, often staying in the facilitators' homes and working together in the classes. Their input was invaluable in ensuring class continuity.

The volunteers had to source funds to purchase books for their students. Many had small cake sales to do this, others approached local businesses for assistance when parents could not contribute. Economies were made by purchasing limited numbers of Reading Books which the students shared. The goal was to have each student have a personal Student Workbook. For the majority of volunteers, many of whom were far from wealthy, there was no option but to dig into their own pockets to provide their students with the materials needed, such as books, pencils, furniture, and a place to hold classes.

RESULTS

As the OWOW initiative evolved, intensive training programmes were undertaken in schools. In one region, in West Coast Demerara in 2006, OWOW formed a variety of partnerships with Saraswat School (475 children participating), Tuschen Majid (21), Uitvlgt School (35), De Willem Health Centre (615) and Meten Meer Zorg Health Centre (44). In all, 98% of participants rated the training 'Excellent' or 'Very good.' Pat Cameron, a literacy expert from Canada, made six trips to Guyana to help develop the programme *(see Box below)*.

In 2009 there were 126 days of OWOW training throughout the country as the programme adopted a regional as opposed to a national training focus thereby increasing the sense of ownership of the intervention. The

Regional Education Officer of one region gave VF written permission to introduce OWOW in all the schools in his region.

One of the significant features of the OWOW programme were the gains seen on standardized test scores. In one region on the West Coast, for example, a total of 474 children were given a baseline Reading Test before the OWOW programme began. Of these 167 children had a deficit in their Reading Age of between 2 and 4 years. Furthermore 92 children had a deficit of seven years or more. A five-month intensive OWOW programme in this region was undertaken. The expected improvement in Reading Age (RA) over the course of the intervention would be of around five months. However, 41% of children made between 6 and 12 months improvement in their Reading Age and 34% made 12 to 24 months improvement. A number of the facilitators recorded, significant attitude change in the children, e.g. new-found courtesy, with anger replaced by calm, increased self-worth and a higher interest in school. Parents began to report about a greater belief in the child's ability, more patience, and enhanced understanding of how to be encouraging with the child.

In 2006 the programme was expanded to include West Bank Demerara with a one-month intensive summer literacy programme run by the OWOW literacy volunteers. In this one-month period, 42 of the 238 children involved in the training saw a 2 to 6-month improvement in their reading ability. Furthermore 102 of the children saw between one and three years of improvement in their reading ability. In all, 35% increased their Reading Age by at least one year, 23% increased by at least two years and 16% increased by between two to six years.

One facilitator reported about a child living with his grandmother, with an alcoholic father and a mother forced into prostitution. The child was accustomed to being beaten in the home. Neither the mother nor the father could see anything good in the child. At the start of the OWOW programme the child was unable to write his own name. However, with the love and encouragement shown by the OWOW facilitator he gradually learnt far more than just writing his own name.

Ms Grant, Ms Horde and Ms Curtis have been working with the Macaw Literacy Group for more than a decade. A young man, Seralie Belfield was one of the students. He went on to study Engineering at the University of Guyana.

RECOGNITION AND RESEARCH

Pam O'Toole, a member of the "On Wings of Words" Task Force, was appointed by the Government of Guyana to the Fast Track Literacy Task Force that had a budget of G$115 million and which planned to work with a total of 13,500 children, youth and adults throughout the country in the school system. This significant sum of money was secured to purchase the OWOW books. However, a fire promptly destroyed all the books. There was then a change of administration in the country and the books were never re ordered.

Funders and Government Ministers however recognized the impact the programme was having. In 2004 VF was given the Inter-American Development Bank Cultural Development in the Field Award. Ms Chapman from the European Union wrote in her report to EU, "wonderful to see how well your project was working ......I don't think I have ever seen such a committed group of workers." (Chapman, 1998).

Dr. Dale Bisnauth, Minister of Education stated, "OWOW is not 'about' the best organized response that we have had in the nation to literacy... OWOW is literally treading new ground ...we have never had anything like this before."

LESSONS LEARNT

A key aspect of the OWOW programme was the number of effective partnerships that were formed. Some of those key partnerships included; the National Rights of the Child Commission, the Guyana Book Foundation and the Caribbean Organisation for Development through Education. Peace Corps included OWOW as an integral part of the training for their new volunteers in Guyana.

OWOW also attracted students from the University of Alberta, and University of Kingston to undertake their service project in Guyana. Dr. Somava Stout undertook her research for her Master's in Development from the University of Berkley on the various VF development projects in the interior of Guyana and Ms Karen Brooks wrote her Master's thesis from the University of Michigan on OWOW.

VF also welcomed a number of Year of Service volunteers to work on the OWOW programme from USA, Canada and UK.

The key role played by the two coordinators needs to be recorded. They demonstrated the importance of the role of accompaniment. Lomeharshan Lall and Rosheni Takechandra travelled extensively throughout the country staying with the participants in their homes, supporting, encouraging and troubleshooting.

A key part of the evolution of the OWOW programme was the movement from national to regional trainings in the hope of promoting sustainability OWOW attempted to develop new facilitation skills, creating a new model of intervention based on problem solving and nurturing rather than the mindless rote learning that was, and is, pervasive in schools and which only deadens the educational experience of the children.

A major challenge for VF in pursuing the various development initiatives was to promote a synergy between them. This proved more challenging than we first expected. Creating a unity of vision grew more complicated as VF added new Lines of Action. In trying to promote sustainability and ownership we lost key momentum. Indeed, it was only when we opened the OWOW to the wider Guyanese community that the programme developed momentum.

OWOW TODAY?

In conclusion however, we have tried to reflect on what happens when there is an attempt to see how Bahá'í principles can be used to effect change in both the physical and spiritual life of the society.

However, in reflecting on the OWOW programme it is easy, with the benefit of hindsight, to forget the challenges of migration, unemployment, poverty and violence that mired so much of Guyana in the 1980s and 1990s. It is against this very harsh background that one needs to reflect why more was not done by the government authorities to secure the gains of the OWOW programme. As outlined above there were sporadic attempts by the authorities in Guyana to incorporate OWOW into mainstream education but such efforts were never sustained. It is now left to School of Nations to continue the work of Varqa Foundation and offer OWOW training to receptive teachers and schools. For the first time perhaps School of Nations has a stronger partnership with the Ministry of Education and a possibility exists to re open possible lines of collaboration. We will need to see if that indeed evolves. For that partnership to blossom will require humility on the part of key players and agencies that a fundamental revision is indeed urgently required. There is also little reason to think that the earlier research by Jennings at the University of Guyana and by Nations Research Institute for British Aid is no longer relevant. Indeed, the challenge of illiteracy may be the biggest challenge facing the education system in Guyana. OWOW surely offers one path.

REFLECTION *by Pat Cameron (Canada)*

On the Wings of Words literacy project has impacted communities at multiple levels by building capacity in cohorts of ordinary people of all ages that enabled them to provide basic literacy instruction in small group, learning settings, both formal and informal. Gathering at auntie's house or under a tree or in a formal school classroom, children throughout Guyana have had their literacy instruction supplemented and strengthened by committed volunteers who have taken a series of training sessions to help them learn how to teach reading. Leveled workbooks and readers, that start at the most basic foundation of introduction of pre-literacy activities, to exposure to alphabet letters and sounds, to phoneme chunks and decoding strategies and instruction in comprehension, have all been developed in Guyana for the Guyanese cultural context. These materials have been put into the hands of people with a desire to improve their villages and neighbourhoods by raising literacy levels of children.

My early association with OWOW began over 20 years ago in 1996, when I was invited to help with some training workshops. Right from the outset I was deeply impressed with the dedication of the team of Bahá'ís and their friends that developed pedagogically appropriate materials for the task of elevating literacy levels from the grassroots, with a vision of empowering anyone with a willingness to help. Hundreds and thousands of volunteers have moved through trainings in how to introduce concepts, provide practice, reinforce skills through games and activities and workbook tasks. They were given opportunities to practice together, support each other, return to future trainings to give and receive feedback, and celebrate successes. People who came to be trained ranged in age from mid-teens to energetic elders who were all concerned about children they knew that were not learning to read well. The workshops were funded externally so that people could attend for free, and when they completed the training they received all the materials they needed to conduct literacy classes in their home communities.

The most inspiring experience I had with OWOW, however, was with the 'target population' of the project – at risk children themselves. OWOW partnered with the International Labour Organization to work with groups of children who were most at risk of leaving school because of a combination of poverty, poor school performance due to illiteracy, and external forces that would lure them into drug and sex trade. A group of OWOW volunteers went regularly to work with Form 1 students who were completely illiterate, using remedial materials to introduce the letters and sounds, the basic building blocks of literacy. I was working with a young woman who had adopted a pattern of being mischievous to mask her illiteracy. We were introducing the letter 'Mm' and the workbook asks learners to circle pictures of things that have the initial sound of 'm'. Working one-on-one with this girl, I demonstrated the task. She watched. Her agitation stopped and her focus became laser. She hesitantly pointed to the picture of a mouse. Yes! Then, she picked Moon. Right again. Mountain. The right answer three times in a row, a rare experience for this girl. She stood up and announced, "This shape says mmmmm! I want to do more" her eyes and smile lit her face, "….More says mmmm!" It was so exciting to see a child unlock the secret of reading – that the symbols make sounds and that sounds have meaning. And linking those concepts is the key to unlocking the prison of failure in school.

On the Wings of Words has given this key to countless numbers of Guyanese children during its tireless existence as a project of School of Nations and the Bahá'í community of Guyana.

CHAPTER 3

Integrated Developments in the Rupununi

Brian O'Toole and Somava Stout

INTRODUCTION

By today's standards it was just a gentle disagreement. The husband and wife were arguing about who had decided to bring their six-year old son on the journey. But this was no ordinary journey – the young couple had just completed a 13 day walk from their home on the Brazilian border to attend our two-day training on health issues in the main village in the Rupununi. This was my first introduction to the Amerindian people of the region and I was reminded of the 'wiser heads' from the capital who had earlier warned me away from working in this region as the Amerindian people 'are not interested in such programmes.' For my part I was just grateful that the two-day workshop was not about time management.

When the Rupununi Project began in 1990 more than 7% of the population of Guyana had accepted the Bahá'í Faith. This ten-year project represented an attempt by Varqa Foundation (VF), a Bahá'í inspired NGO, to see what it might mean to try and translate some of the key principles of the Bahá'í Faith into the context of development in one of the most isolated and remote regions of Guyana.

In our efforts to promote 'development' in Guyana we have drawn inspiration from the following definition of human development as offered by the UNDP;

"Human development is all about human freedoms: freedom to realize the full potential of every human life, not just of a few, nor of most, but of all lives in every corner of the world—now and in the future. Such universalism

The hope for the future in Rupununi

gives the human development approach its uniqueness." UNDP (2016) Human Development Report 2016: Human Development for Everyone.

Looking back, our initial efforts to translate that definition into practice were quite limited. They included a number of visits from health professionals from UK, Canada and USA, many of whom came from the Bahá'í inspired agency, Health for Humanity. The focus was on providing much needed health supplies and renovations of hospitals in the capital and rural areas.

This chapter traces the evolution of the project from a traditional model of well intentioned, Western 'assistance', to an attempt to explore deeper issues of collaboration and partnership with native Amerindian people in the second poorest country in the Americas. The chapter will provide

Page 10   MIRROR, Sunday September 25 , 199

Facts For Life Festival In Lethem

On September 17-18, representatives from almost every village in the Rupununi gathered in Lethem for the final of the 'Facts for Life Festival'. The Festival was a joint project of the Guyana Community Based Rehabilitation Programme (CBR), the Baha'i Health Partnership in the Rupununi and UNICEF.

Facts for Life is a book on primary health care messages produced by UNICEF, UNESCO and the World Health Organization. The book contains key health information that could save the lives of millions of people worldwide. The challenge however, is to see how to communicate that information to the grassroots. Over the past year, the Guyana Community Based Rehabilitation Programme and the Baha'i Health Partnership have been collaborating in the Rupununi to take that information to all the homes in the region. The promotion of the information from the book **Facts for Life** has been one of the major objectives of Dr. Jamshid Aidun as he has travelled throughout the region working with the Community Health Workers.

The book contains information on key areas such as malaria, coughs and colds, home hygiene, breast feeding and timing births. Through sponsorship from UNICEF, the Guyana CBR Programme and the Baha'i Health Partnership have produced a 50-minute video, filmed in the Rupununi, based on **Facts for Life**. In addition, in consultation with the Community Health Workers, Teachers and Village leaders in the region, a 70-page illustrated teaching manual has been produced which information is now being shared with people of all ages in the region.

A series of sub-regional festivals regions were then presented at the Rupununi finals held over the weekend of September 17-18.

The competition was sponsored by UNICEF and the trophies donated by National Bank of Industry and Commerce (NBIC). Throughout the weekend, representatives from over 30 villages in the Rupununi presented their cultural items.

UNICEF was represented at the Festival by Mr. Mike Hamid and Ms. Eppie Mfundo. Dr. Ruddy Cummings, Director of Regional Health Services and Nurse Roberts represented the Ministry of Health. The Festival was opened by the Regional Chairperson, Mr. Eustace Rodrigues.

The winners in the Festival are as follows:

(a) Poems: 6-9 years: 'Personal Hygiene' by Lynthia Bremner, Lethem; 10-14 years: 'Hygiene' by Stanislaus Leo, Youron Perud; 15-18 years: 'Timing Births' - Elroy Roberts, Yupukari; 19 years +: 'Health Growth': by Edna Rodney, Annai.

(b) Posters: 6-9 years: Mac Lean Benjamin, Yakarinta; 10-14 years: Jacqueline Johnny, Yakarinta, 15-18 years: Ken Grant, St Ignatius; 19 years + : G. Murray, Karasabai.

(c) Stories: 'Preventing Malaria' by Serena Marco, Karasabai; 15-18 years: 'Malaria' by Ken Grant, St. Ignatius; 19 years +: 'Diarrhoea' by Rudolph Robets, Yupukari.

(d) Skits, over years category: CBR Group from Annai.

(e) Songs, over 19 years: 'Breast milk is the Best' by Vitalis Alfred, Awarenau.

The weekend also featured the Second Rupununi CBR Conference and gathered together over 80 CBR workers from throughout the region. The programme featured contributa presentation of a comprehensive disability survey of the entire region. On the second day Drs. Cummings, Khan and Aidun presented ideas on how the general public can work in partnership with the health personnel in producing a healthier environment.

In a similar way, three head teachers, Mr Elmo Pernambuco, Ms Edna Rodney and Mr Winston Pugsley spoke on wider partnerships within the field of education. Continuing the theme of working together, Ms Laureen Pierre spoke on the collaboration in the region between the CBR Programme and the Baha'i Health Partnership. Reports were then submitted from the 5 sub-regions on the work achieved by the various CBR teams over the past year. The CBR Conference then concluded with par-

Photo was taken of those participating in the Rupununi gathering.

ticipants reflecting on the challenges to be faced over the coming year. The two CBR co-ordinators, Dr. O'Toole and Ms Cynthia Massay, listened carefully to the presentations from the various regions.

The CBR Conference and the Facts for Life Festival are examples of an effective partnership which has been forged in the Rupununi region between the Guyana CBR Programme, the Baha'i Health Partnership, the Ministry of Health, the Ministry of Education and the Regional Administration.

Mirror Newspaper, Sept. 25th 1994

an overview of the project and explore what lessons about integrated development may have emerged that could be of relevance to others. We examine some of the 'successes', but, more importantly, explore the challenges faced on that decade-long journey to try to understand a little more of what a new model of development might look like.

SITUATIONAL ANALYSIS: RUPUNUNI:

The Rupununi, a land of 33,000 square miles, lies in the South West corner of Guyana, bordering Brazil. The population of 17,000 persons live in 42 scattered and isolated villages. Around 80% of the population are indigenous Amerindians whose lives have changed little over centuries. The Rupununi represents one of the ten administrative regions of Guyana. Whilst many decisions are made centrally, because of its remoteness there is some degree of autonomy in terms of administration.

The population density is one person for every three-square kilometers. The Rupununi is the second poorest region of Guyana. Neighbouring Brazil attracts great numbers from this region, further depleting the economic and human resources. The Rupununi that we met in 1990 was largely a land of cultural erosion, few of the inhabitants could read or write their traditional languages, and their rich cultural heritage, their songs, stories and art were fast being forgotten.

In 1990, 20% of all the girls in the region who were aged between 15 and 19 were already mothers. The crude mortality rate was 2.9%, infant mortality was 35/1000 live births and the region had the highest rate of low birth weights in the country: 42% of infants born were less than 2.5 kg in weight. The Rupununi was the only part of the country where leishmaniosis, tuberculosis, conjunctivitis were still significant health problems. Around 25% of the under-fives were not immunized.

Prevailing agriculture, on the nutrient-poor soil, was, and still is, almost entirely subsistence farming resulting in very limited cash flow in the region. There was a high turnover of administrators in the area with the average nurse/midwife staying in the region for no more than one year.

Because of transportation barriers (bullock carts and bicycles were the primary transportation vehicles on dirt roads,) and communication barriers (CB radio was then the only means of communication between villages), there was therefore very little sharing of insight or resources between villages.

In 1990 only 10% of elected village officials were women. Every year there was, if the region was lucky, a Regional Health Officer (RHO) assigned to administer to the health needs of the region. However, the RHO was invariably someone from outside the region who often didn't want to be there and didn't have a good sense of what to do to create improvement or have trust with the local indigenous community.

Rupununi in the 1980s and 1990s had therefore long been neglected by development projects. Indeed, when we began plans for this project we were warned away by administrators from the capital who informed us saying that it was simply too difficult a region to 'effect change' and anyway 'the people there don't want to change'.

This programme began with a plan to phase itself out within ten years. The programme leaders saw untapped potential and believed in the ability of the local and regional Amerindian community to develop the capacity to take over the process of development for themselves.

The statistics and negative appraisals however overlook the greatest resource of the region: the people. The Rupununi villagers probably did not know the development terminology such as 'community ownership, empowerment and participation', but their very lives were founded on exactly those principles. For centuries they had relied on locally initiated and implemented solutions to community problems.

A decade later we realised how very wrong the initial advice from the capital was and how misleading the statistics were.

EARLY STEPS AT INTRODUCING AN INTEGRATED DEVELOPMENT PROJECT

CBR IN THE RUPUNUNI

I had been working on a Community Based Rehabilitation (CBR) disability project in several coastal regions of Guyana, for about six years before the intervention in the Rupununi began. The challenge in the Rupununi was to see whether attempting to respond to disability within this demanding environment could be a realistic proposition. CBR is based on the theory that someone from the community should be trained to develop individualised rehabilitation programmes for persons with disabilities. CBR seeks to demystify the rehabilitation process and give responsibility back to the individual, family and community. The hope is to see rehabilitation as part of community development, whereby the community seeks to improve itself. Rehabilitation then becomes one element of a broader community development initiative.

In 1990 an attempt was made to expand the Guyana CBR programme, for children with disabilities, into the Rupununi. I was invited to speak at a Conference that was being held for all the Head Teachers in the Rupununi. The Heads Teachers listened respectfully, as is the Amerindian way, and then simply reported that "there were no persons with disability in the region."

There followed visits to 20 of the 42 villages in the region, over a 40-day period, to meet with the villagers and get a sense of the perceived needs of the various communities. In each village, a public meeting was organised introducing our team to the community and providing a forum for the villagers to express what they felt their needs to be.

Our team at that stage was simply Laureen Pierre and myself. We were fortunate that a key member of our team was Laureen, herself an Amerindian, who was known and respected throughout the region. Laureen facilitated those early meetings and because of the trust she had already earned the villagers soon voiced their concerns.

Amongst the major needs identified in the 20 villages were; improved water and sanitation, training in health and education, community education on alcohol abuse, training in literacy, better agriculture and improved health centres.

The reader can judge at the end of the chapter, how well, if at all, we responded to these challenges. It should be noted too, not surprisingly, that there was not one mention of disability as a perceived need in any of the 20 villages consulted.

In October of 1992, the CBR team organised two, one week, workshops for Community Health Workers (CHWs) in collaboration with the Ministry of Health on topics such as early stimulation, identification of children with special needs, and toy and puppet making. That was the workshop where the couple walked 13 days in each direction to attend and, very early on, we were forced to reflect on the negative reports we had been given on the region that 'no one would be interested'. But at that first workshop too we also met all the Community Health Workers (CHWs) and heard that almost all of them had lost a child, or children, of their own to simple, treatable, diarrhoea.

Because of the enthusiastic response from the CHWs in the region, the administrators of the CBR team then met with the funders of the CBR programme, Amici di Raoul Follereau (AIFO) in Italy, to explore ways in which the CBR programme could be expanded in this isolated and remote region.

In each village, a team of three persons was identified to form a CBR team, comprised of a teacher, the CHW and a village leader. This helped to develop a unified model of training and was in fact the first joint training in the region for health workers and educators together. The training created a sense of ownership and identification with the programme. The CBR team members in turn shared what they learnt at their regular village meetings. The initial training focussed on early stimulation and making toys out of locally available materials, which, in turn, was an affirmation of Amerindian resources and culture.

The second series of workshops focussed on child development, and simple ways to increase awareness within the community of the needs of children with disabilities. Ideas were shared on how to carry out a survey of children with special needs in the villages. This resulted in children with disabilities being identified, who, up to that point had been hidden away at home. Twenty of these children were later integrated into the regular schools in the region. The CBR teams helped to integrate persons with disabilities into mainstream community life. For example, mothers were encouraged to take their children with special needs to the Village Health Centres, many for the first time.

The third series of workshops saw a breakthrough with one of the CBR teams bringing seven persons with disabilities to the workshop. The workshop then spontaneously reflected on how many other such persons were in the region and what could be done to help them. The 42 villages of the region were divided into 5 sub regions. In each sub region an additional 4-day workshop was held.

One significant development was that a team of twelve persons from the Rupununi then went to an intensive, two-week, training in the capital to learn how to become the facilitators of a similar training in two neighbouring and very isolated Amerindian regions – the Pakaraimas and the North-West District.

The village CBR teams began to formulate their own plans rather than simply reacting to suggestions from 'experts'. They began to own the process and see themselves as agents rather than as recipients of the intervention. A three-prong focus began to emerge beyond the CBR project, based on:

- Health education
- Literacy training
  and
- Cultural affirmation

HEALTH EDUCATION

Our journey as health educators had an unlikely beginning. We were in an Italian restaurant in London with Dr. Farzin Rahmani, a UK based anaesthetist. Over copious deserts we decided to 'start a health project in Guyana.' This resulted in a two week visit by two UK doctors, Farzin Rahmani and Rustom Behesti, to offer their services to the people of Guyana. The National Spiritual Assembly, a body of nine elected Bahá'ís from the country, helped in the planning of this visit. At the time both my wife and I served on this body.

The Assembly decided to host a large meeting for the prominent persons in the country to introduce the two doctors to Guyana. As we were formulating the plans we received a call saying the Prime Minister of Guyana wished to address that meeting. The night of the meeting saw more than 300 of Guyana's most prominent persons gathered at the National Cultural Centre. The Prime Minister, as the opening speaker, looked around the audience and suddenly announced, "Really this is almost a waste of time …. More than 300 of you have gathered here and for what…. Two doctors are here from UK for less than 2 weeks … what can be done in that time?" But then the Prime Minister continued, "but the Bahá'í community has the potential to make a profound impact on this country." The next day the headline in the national newspaper was a quote from the Prime Minister, "The Bahá'ís show what religion is all about."

MAKING A START

Varqa Foundatin (VF) was a well-established Bahá'í inspired NGO based in the capital. The Bahá'í Community Health Partnership (BCHP) was the name given to the integrated development project in the Rupununi.

As the programme evolved, VF formed a strong partnership with Health for Humanity (HH) whereby a number of health professionals, largely from North America, came to the Rupununi to support the programme for periods of one to two weeks. They assisted in a variety of ways including training, programme development and material resources. For example, the Regional Hospital was totally renovated with equipment procured by HH in the USA. In the early days that concern was channelled into organising a shipment of a container load of medical supplies to the National Hospital. But gradually the vision widened.

A visit to the Rupununi region by a senior person from the European Union (EU) led to a request to the Bahá'í community to see what help could be offered in the Rupununi as there was no doctor resident in the entire region. The EU person had been shocked to learn of the near-death of one pregnant lady who was forced to travel miles in a bullock cart to arrive at the poorly equipped Regional Hospital to deliver her baby.

This led in 1992 to a Canadian surgeon, Dr. Jamshid Aidun, offering to settle in the Rupununi to promote what became the 'Bahá'í Community Health Partnership' (BCHP). CIDA – the Canadian International Development Agency - provided a Land Rover to help Dr. Aidun reach all parts of the region.

At that time in the Rupununi there was a regional hospital with eight beds but little else: no blood bank, laboratory, or anaesthesia. Dr. Aidun began to rehabilitate the hospital with the support of Health for Humanity. But, it quickly became apparent that most people simply couldn't get to the hospital. It took 6 to 24 hours by bullock cart, depending on where you lived.

Every village was then visited by Dr. Aidun every six weeks. His main focus was to develop preventative health services. Initially he focussed on health promotion, health education, family planning, immunization and malaria screening. Links were established with existing health care initiatives; the Maternal and Child Health programme of the Ministry of Health, Malaria Control, Ministry of Education and the other one or two NGOs operating in the region. In 1992 there were however only a handful of serviceable vehicles in the entire region and whilst 'services' existed in the region it was often very difficult for them to be able to travel to the villages to take the interventions to those in need. The BCHP vehicle was therefore crucial in this regard.

I remember early on in the project accompanying Dr. Aidun and the Community Health Worker to the home of a lady suffering from malaria. Dr. Aidun, a surgeon with 40 years' experience, asked the CHW to examine the lady and gently questioned him on what course of treatment he recommended. Deep respect for local communities in creating their own futures was demonstrated in different ways throughout the project.

With prevention in mind, the programme brought together existing assets: a nurse midwife who administered the vaccines and family planning for the region, the malaria control worker, and the physician. A key aspect of Dr. Aidun's work was supporting the 36 Community Health Workers (CHWs) in the region. The CHWs had a modest three months of training after High School from the government and were then sent out to care for their communities.

As the BCHP developed over time and we began to appreciate what was needed in the region, the programme further evolved: supporting public health campaigns, art competitions and engaging thousands of people in the region to own their own health and preventive care. Water wells got covered, latrines built, and nursery schools established.

Village Health Boards (VHB) were elected in 24 of the villages, without canvassing or electioneering. The purpose of the VHB was to provide a forum at which village leaders could consult on the many challenges facing their community. The members of the VHBs were then invited to attend a series of two-day workshops on consultation skills, moral leadership, the concept of service and conflict resolution. These VHBs went on to play a key role in the development of the BCHP by taking on a clear sense of ownership of the intervention.

The VHBs were challenged to think more broadly about what "health" means and began to respond to the WHO challenge of seeing health as, "complete physical, mental and social wellbeing." The development of a new style of moral leadership was emerging. Over time, the people in the region began to see the development of health and wellbeing as something that required local ownership of health as a shared value across sectors.

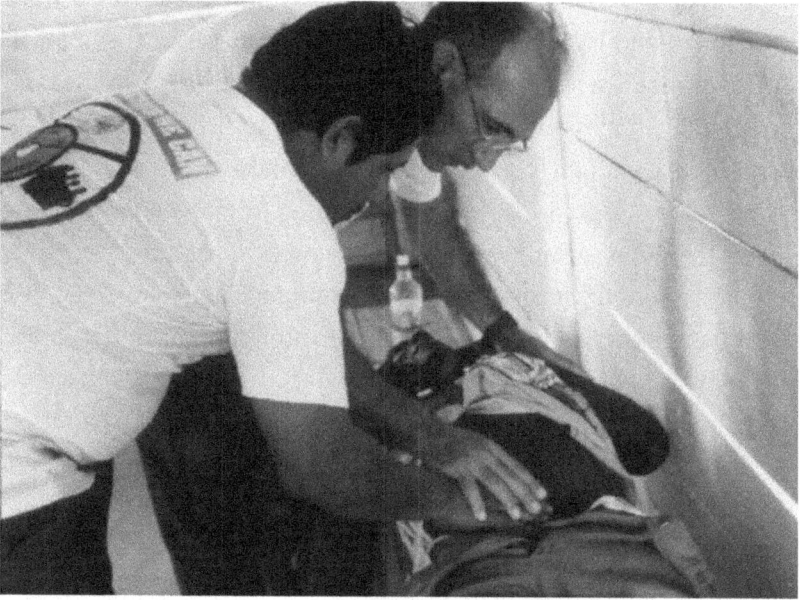

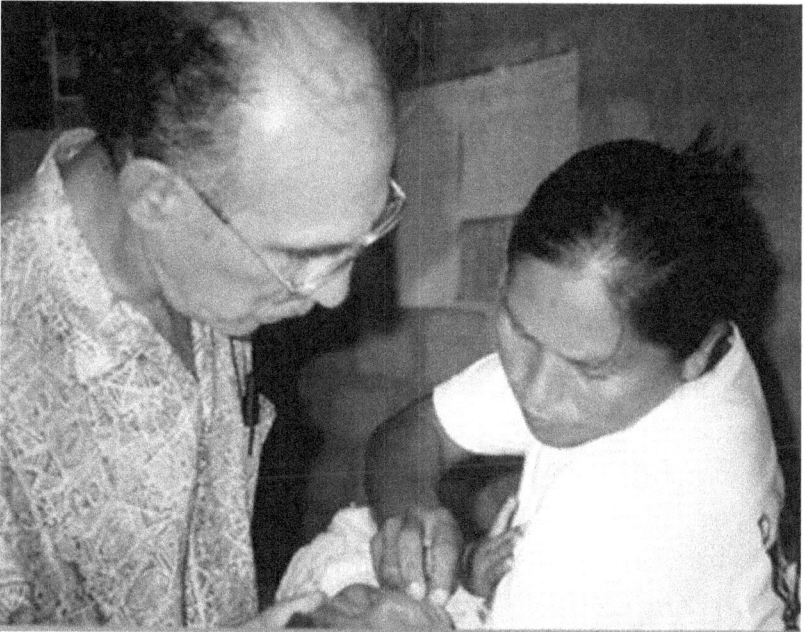

Dr. Aidun at work in the Rupunini

Innovations blossomed using solutions that could only have been developed and implemented by local people because they had the trust to share assets across sectors. In one village, the VHB, in assessing their community, realised that widows were malnourished because they could not produce enough food from farming to make it through the dry season. In the same village, 80% of villagers suffered from malaria every year. They knew that they could prevent malaria with mosquito nets, but simply couldn't afford these in a subsistence economy. Members of the VHB spoke with the widows and convinced them to stop farming and instead form a sewing cooperative to weave mosquito nets that they could barter for food with local villagers. Within a year, the incidence of malaria had dropped by 90% and malnutrition among widows was eliminated.

Another CHW noted that children in the region were exhibiting a developmental delay by the time they were five years old. At that time, there was no concept of playing with or talking with infants in the Amerindian culture. The CHW developed a parent-run nursery school and taught mothers to play with their children, using locally available resources to make puppets and build playgrounds. These ideas spread throughout the region and within three years, they had nearly eliminated acquired developmental delay.

A key element of the BCHP was translating the messages from the UNICEF publication, 'Facts for Life' into practice. A video, filmed entirely in the Rupununi, was made of the key messages from the book. The video was subsequently shown in 32 of the villages throughout the region. It was accompanied by a series of health pamphlets. 'Facts for Life' Festivals were then held in all five sub districts with the villagers putting the key health messages into poems, songs, posters and skits. A Regional 'Facts for Life' Festival was organised with all the winning entries from the sub-regions. UNICEF published an illustrated book featuring all the winning entries. This proved to be an empowering process for the Village Health Workers. Likewise, an art competition highlighting the challenges of children with special needs, attracted hundreds of entries with every village submitting pieces.

Over time, as the VHBs gained confidence, they began taking on structural change. They realized that having only up to a fifth-grade education substantially limited their ability to control the fate of their health system. The VHBs (which by this time had elected a Regional Health Assembly) decided to invest in building a stronger secondary school program with a well-developed science curriculum.

Within ten years, they increased the number of physicians, nurses, midwives and science workers within the region. People in the Rupununi learned to tell funders interested in investing in the region to support local initiatives and priorities rather than pushing their own agendas. VHBs worked with eco-tourist and development agencies to build roads to help address economic isolation. Because they had strong community and regional leadership involved in the decisions they were able to do this in a way that promoted local initiatives, culture, and economy.

Throughout this period, the Varqa Foundation team continued to accompany the Village Health Boards, building capacity, helping them to step back and reflect, and supporting the teams to overcome barriers and spread good ideas. They described this model of providing assistance as "accompaniment": walking alongside a group, trusting in their growth in leadership and capacity over time, providing the support that is needed during different phases as the relationship evolves to one of full partnership and eventually full leadership by local people.

The BCHP programme began to earn the reputation of responding to the needs as articulated by the community and, unlike so many, as one CHW said, "they kept their promises".

LITERACY

The need for help in promoting literacy was repeatedly reinforced at the initial community meetings. Over the course of the next ten years, workshops were held to not only train all the teachers in the Rupununi region, but to train many of the villagers too. English is the medium of instruction in the schools even though in most of the homes the indigenous language of that area is used.

This training led to the creation of the 'Steps to Reading' programme, developed by Pamela O'Toole, that included a 15-book series with workbooks and teacher's manuals and story books which take teachers, step by step, through the process of promoting literacy. It should be noted that this programme that emerged out of the Rupununi went on to form the basis of the On the Wings of Words literacy programme that was to train more than 4,000 literacy facilitators throughout Guyana and which went on to inspire literacy initiatives in other parts of the world.

This literacy training in the Rupununi was recognised and certified by the Extra Mural Department of the University of Guyana and constituted the first time the University had a presence in the region.

The first, CBR literacy training workshop was attended by all the teachers of the Rupununi and focussed on the promotion of literacy and numeracy skills. All the logistical arrangements for the training were undertaken by the Regional Education Department of the Rupununi.

The CBR programme collaborated with a Bahá'í community in Dundas, Canada to arrange the donation of 24,000 books to the region. The Varqa Foundation team in the capital then sorted through all the books and arranged the transportation to the villages in the Rupununi. The books had been secured from school libraries in Ontario. The Varqa team screened the books so that titles like 'The Maritime Laws of the Great Lakes' did not make the journey into the Rupununi. The great majority of the easy fiction books however proved to be invaluable. The CBR team then worked with Varqa Foundation to establish libraries in 24 of the 42 villages in the Rupununi. Many of these libraries were placed in schools and in almost all cases this was the first time those schools had a library. In 18 of these villages this was the first time that the village had a library. The CBR programme and the Bahá'í community then worked with the Canadian Office of Development through Education (CODE) to train librarians for each of the communities. Dr. Aidun's Land Rover was then used over time to rotate the books between the various libraries. Over the next few years a high percentage of the population of the region used these libraries.

CULTURAL AFFIRMATION

A major focus within the programme was to respect the culture of the region at each step of the various innovations.

A video series, 'A New Tomorrow,' was produced in the Rupununi and featured ways to stimulate child development in the preschool years. These materials were later purchased by CBR programmes in 44 countries and translated into Spanish, Portuguese, Italian, Arabic, Farsi and Amharic. A book of children's stories, was written by persons from the community, and translated into the major languages of the region, Macushi and Wapishiana.

Workshops were conducted in every village on puppet and toy making, using locally available materials. Story and art competitions were held thereby enhancing the programme by drawing on inspiration from their own culture and environment.

The CBR programme arranged for a professional music-ethnographer from Canada to record the music, songs and stories of the villagers, much of which was on the verge of being lost. For more than 100 years the people of the region had been beaten for speaking their indigenous languages. This was one attempt to affirm the integrity and value of their culture.

Pamela O'Toole produced a video and educational material on the rainforest, helping children on the coast to appreciate the majesty and potential of the region. This was supported by story books on 'Waldorf the Water Drop' to help children understand water as an essential resource.

LESSONS LEARNT

The CBR and BCHP programmes attracted a series of local and international evaluations and media coverage such as Vision TV in Canada that produced a 25-minute documentary of the programme that was watched by thousands of persons in North America. Dr. Somava Stout based her Master's Thesis from the University of Berkley on both the CBR and BCHP interventions. Some of the key success factors these evaluators identified are summarised in the Box. But we want to highlight the main lessons we learnt from our work in the Rupununi.

KEY SUCCESS FACTORS FOR SUSTAINABLE, INTEGRATED COMMUNITY DEVELOPMENT

- The need for a broad, shared vision of health and wellbeing that is owned as everyone's responsibility within the community.
- A deep belief in the ability of local communities to create their own future and solutions.
- Viewing the process of development as unlocking the trapped and untapped potential of local people and communities to create the solutions they need, and believing in their ability to create effective solutions.
- A focus on partnership as core to success, and valuing unity in diversity for what each partner contributes.
- An instilled belief in interconnectedness of people within and across communities and focused on building culture as well as technical skills.
- An accompaniment model of support by the technical assistance provider, which required significant reinvention of support to provide "just-in-time" skills and support to match what the community was trying to accomplish.
- The belief that community members, even with a fifth-grade education, could acquire the skills to assess what was needed in their community, identify the community's strengths, develop improvements, and test them in measurable ways to see whether the changes led to improvement.
- Embrace system transformation in practical ways.

FAITH AND RESPECT FOR RURAL PERSONS

The goal of the programme was to help persons bring about change in their own condition and take more responsibility for their own affairs. An exciting element of the CBR and BCHP programmes was the Training of Trainers model that was adopted. One element of this was the introduction of the programme into neighbouring Amerindian regions. A selected group from the Rupununi CBR team members attended a two-week workshop in the capital to learn how to facilitate this process. The workshop focussed on the promotion of literacy, health education and disability. They were given on-the-job training to practice their newly acquired skills to apply, develop and gain confidence in their new skills. The CBR and BCHP programmes therefore raised human resources from one region to work in two other Amerindian areas. Persons from the Rupununi region had never been used in this way before.

The goal was to nurture and reinforce the efforts rather than supplant the authority of teachers, health workers and community leaders. The hope was to raise up resources from within the community and not via external agents and to help the community see the role they are playing

Villagers gather to meet Dr Aidun

in developing their community. Before the people of the region were perceived as poor passive recipients of what others would donate. As one CBR worker commented however, "We have now been encouraged to do something, to help ourselves... this is a self-help programme, ... we have learnt we can do something." Persons began to play a more active role in their own development. The CBR and BCHP programmes gave persons from the community the opportunity to put into practice their fundamental desire to be of service to others.

Each CBR team was asked to organise a workshop themselves in their own village on early stimulation. They were given a refresher course on this topic. They learnt how to teach others, therefore they became active participants in the education process.

PROMOTION OF AN INTEGRATED MODEL OF DEVELOPMENT

The programme worked across sectors to arrive at an integrated model of community development. Amongst the diverse achievements of the CBR and BCHP teams are the following: establishing nursery schools, upgrading health posts, improving water and sanitation by building wells, establishing cooperatives to sew mosquito nets and seeking external funding for their own projects

DEVELOPMENT NEEDS TO BE IN HARMONY WITH THE LOCAL CULTURE

As much time as possible was invested in listening to the people of the region. The CBR programme began by focussing on early stimulation and child development practices which reflected their culture. Festivals of poetry and art were promoted throughout the region. At each stage of the programme time was invested in gaining the support of local officials.

PROMOTION OF UNITY

Both the CBR and BCHP programmes established partnerships between the health and education services of the region which normally worked separately. Too often NGOs unknowingly supplant and disempower existing government systems. This intervention sought to support government personnel working at the base of the health and education systems.

CONSULTATION

The guiding principle throughout this programme was the attempt to engender open and equitable consultation. Villagers were encouraged to discuss community concerns. We tried to listen carefully and then act on what we heard. There was no script at the outset. Actions emerged out of the consultations. Such a process takes time and cannot be hurried. A flexible and responsive approach was adopted to the suggestions from the community.

WIDER REPLICABILITY?

This intervention could be introduced elsewhere if certain conditions are respected. The innovators have to firmly believe in the potential of the people they are serving. They need to guide persons who for so long have traditionally been led by others to take charge of their own affairs. They also need to nurture the active participation of those involved at all phases of the innovation and to be able to listen carefully to people who may at first appear not to be articulate. Funders need to allow enough time to facilitate such a process. In both the BCHP and CBR programmes there was no predetermined script. Many of the most creative features emerged from the participants over time.

DEVELOPMENT OF AN APPROPRIATE INFRASTRUCTURE

Village Health Boards and CBR Committees played a central role in the programme. The responsibility for the programme was transferred back into the hands of the community. Persons learnt how to identify a need, make plans to meet that need and carry out plans in an efficient, empowering and unified way.

The CBR and BCHP programmes were integrated into an existing village and regional system. Resource persons were drawn from the existing health and education infrastructure and the necessary regional and national bodies were committed from the outset. At the regular meetings of head teachers, CBR featured on the agenda. VHB reports were submitted to the Regional Health authorities. The Ministry of Health report of 1994 stated (pp120) "increased access to rehabilitation care by introducing CBR as the main strategy for delivering rehabilitation services at the primary care level."

CONCLUSION

In summary, at the heart of this programme were a number of key principles including:

- a profound respect for the community
- the practice of open and equitable consultation as an integral part of the development process.
- the need to avoid any creation of dependency and seek to promote sustainability
- recognition that local communities should be encouraged and trained to assume responsibility for as much of the project as possible.
- realisation that change in development terms takes time and involves change in human values

A main contribution of this project was the nurturing of these key principles many of which required a culture shift to be put into operation.

There is a need to promote a process of study, action and reflection. An essential feature of this process will be the need to foster the capacity of persons to learn to work together and to begin to appreciate the role of the 'leader' as 'accompanying' others and understanding the dynamics of organisational development. The key here will be to learn in action, through a process of reflection, study and consultation and consider skills and spiritual insights that lay the foundation for personal and social change.

WHAT REMAINS OF THIS PROGRAMME YEARS LATER?

'Sustainability' is the touchstone of all development programmes. Translating that mantra into practice is considerably more difficult. However, local communities took responsibility for the innovations through the Village Health Boards and the village based CBR Committees. The community was involved in all phases of the programme.

Efforts to promote sustainability included; developing a clear match between local needs and programme objectives, using the existing health and education infrastructures rather than creating a new cadre of workers, the management of the programme being based within the region and the focus throughout was on involving and empowering the community

The BCHP and Varqa Foundation team crucially planned from the inception to transition out of the region within about ten years, but continued to provide remote coaching and training as needed.

The goal from the inception was to avoid dependency and to help persons in the community begin to take control of their own lives and to appreciate the nobility of their own culture and the fact that their voices needed to be heard and respected. As the intervention developed the villagers began to see the programmes at theirs, they became the key actors in the process rather than being passive spectators as they had been for so long.

Gradually the intervention began to translate into practice the flourishing vocabulary of community developers: namely empowerment, ownership, participation. No doubt, few of the Amerindians knew these terms but the programme was now theirs and they were unquestionably the key players. Dr. Somava Stout in undertaking her Master's Thesis based on this programme concluded that the entire region had been transformed as a result of this intervention. Years later, the key players in the region in the area of health, the doctors, nurses and medexes, are almost all native to the region. This is highlighted in the following reflection by Dr. Aidun. In this sense therefore the programme can be seen to have fulfilled its objectives.

The Rupununi team

REFLECTION *by Dr. Jamshid Aidun*

A key aspect of the BCHP was the formation of the Village Health Boards. After they were elected we had a series of workshops with them on such topics as consultation, problem solving, developing a vision and team building. They then undertook a range of projects in their own communities including: purification of the water supply, covering of wells and building latrines. When Vision TV came to film a documentary on the BCHP, one of the CHWs in his interview said he hoped to become a doctor. At the time we thought about editing that out of the final film as it seemed so unrealistic. Ten years later, he is a doctor working in the Rupununi.

In 2004 I was invited by the Minister of Health to return to work in the Rupununi. However, I told the Minister that I was getting old and that Guyana needed to invest in training the people from the community. On my last trip to the Rupununi seven of the doctors that I met were local Amerindians from the Rupununi. I was so happy when I returned to Rupununi, my home for so many years, to see the people from the area who were now in charge of their own development.

REFLECTION *by Laureen Pierre*

The ground work for the CBR programme in several coastal communities in Guyana was well laid when I joined as a coordinator for the Rupununi region in 1994. My initial reservations concerning a region-wide community based program in the Rupununi were shaped by my own work and research experience in this part of Guyana. I understood that the geographic features, cultural characteristics and socio-economic circumstances of the Rupununi posed special challenges for effective development undertakings among the Indigenous populations of that area.

CBR activities in the Rupununi moved steadily along at first, but increased significantly as certain concepts of development gained currency and CBR volunteer teams engaged with their communities. Funding for the CBR programme in the Rupununi was critical for covering the expenses associated with training workshops and the support and mentoring of CBR teams in each village. In time, the CBR collaboration with the regional administrative bodies and local agencies increased and the level of commitment and involvement of the villages deepened. As the CBR programme began to receive reports about ways in which individuals, families and communities were transforming their lives, I became convinced that the CBR programme had identified some important strategies for unleashing individual and team energy and creativity, and that the CBR approach offered positive lessons for community development among Guyana's Indigenous Peoples. On one occasion I served as a member of an evaluation team for the CBR project. This exercise allowed me to appreciate the extent to which the CBR programme had impacted the lives of individuals and families with special needs in the Rupununi and in the coastal communities where CBR was active. From my participation in the annual CBR conferences, I came to recognize also that the CBR coordinators, facilitators and volunteers had together cultivated a strong organizational culture. At these conferences they unreservedly shared the learning processes and methodologies that they espoused and employed, encouraged the spirit of nurturing and mentoring, and demonstrated a genuine respect for cultural values.

By the time I left the shores of Guyana in 1999, I had witnessed with pride, trained CBR facilitators from the Rupununi conducting a CBR workshop in the Barima/Waini Region of Guyana. I was also keenly aware that the National CBR Committee, still in its infancy, was grappling with maintaining the momentum of an exciting and expanding CBR programme even as funding and management of the project were shifting in new directions.

CHAPTER 4

Youth Can Move The World - A Youth Leadership Programme in Guyana

Brian O'Toole

Investing in youth is an investment in the future of the nation. Yet this truism is frequently forgotten in many countries around the world, especially for young people leaving school. Internationally the ongoing challenge is how best to engage and enthuse youth on moral and ethical issues. The Youth Can Move the World (YCMTW) programme was our attempt in Guyana to meet this challenge. It grew out of the work that Varqa Foundation (VF) had undertaken in the interior area of Guyana in the Rupununi, Region #9. The VF coordinators had travelled to 12 of the 36 villages in the Rupununi to meet with groups of youth to learn of their concerns. The same process was undertaken on the coast of Guyana to identify the topics that the youth leadership programme, YCMTW, needed to focus on. From small beginnings, it spread across the country reaching thousands of youth and arguably changed many lives. For instance: we had just finished one of the Youth Can Move the World training sessions when a young lady who was part of the programme came up to me to say she was thinking of committing suicide that weekend. Thankfully she didn't. She went on to become one of the most dedicated of all the YCMTW facilitators.

YCMTW training session

CHALLENGES FACING YOUTH IN GUYANA

- In 2006 more than 40% of the youth in Guyana were unemployed.
- 34% of young people, aged 16-25, lived in poverty and almost half of all children aged 16 and below were poor.
- About 18% of the children in Guyana were involved in child labour
- 15% of girls between ages 15 and 19 in Guyana had begun child bearing, with different rates depending on the area that the girl lives, her poverty status, and her ethnicity.
- Only 13% of sexually active adolescents mentioned using contraceptives in their sexual relationships.
- Most of the new cases of HIV/AIDs among children are found between 15 and 19 year old boys and girls.
- Less than 50% of the adolescent population between 15 and 19 years of age (48% for women, and 33% for men) have comprehensive knowledge on HIV and AIDS.
- In 2014, 70% of children reported that they were suffering from some sort of corporal punishment. Common causes of corporal punishment are due to the excessive use of alcohol and drugs, family conflict, and lack of parents' knowledge on other forms of discipline.

Despite the signing by Guyana of a number of international conventions, UNICEF (2016) believes that the failure to implement legislation is one of the major problems in the country in relation to the health, education and child protection of children and young people *(see box above).*

Children living in single-parent households, especially those headed by women, are common in Guyana. These family arrangements are in part driven by the harsh economic situation that pushes parents, mainly men, to search for jobs abroad or in the most remote mining and logging areas of the country.

A major challenge for the youth of Guyana is poverty. Although not all poor families are going to have their children out-of-school, or will have

Youth Can Move the World training sessions

cases of domestic violence, statistically, poor families in Guyana have higher chances of living in a worse-off situation. Children living in poor families have smaller chances of having access to computers and books; they are more susceptible to domestic violence and other types of abuses; they have higher chances of being stunted and have higher chances of being out of school. Poverty is at the core of most, if not all, the problems that affect children and adolescents in Guyana.

In 2006 Guyana had the second highest incidence of HIV/AIDS in the Caribbean, and AIDS was considered the second leading cause of death in the country. Knowledge is one of the most important components in avoiding HIV transmission. Knowledge on mother-to-child HIV transmission is also low in the country (53% among women, and 35% among men), increasing the risk of HIV transmission among those babies born to women who did not have proper prenatal care. Moreover the efficiency of the Prevention of Mother to Child Transmission programme in Guyana is affected by a shortage of essential commodities, difficulty of access to health facilities, financial constraints, and social and cultural practices and beliefs. Deficiencies in the prenatal care, delivery and postnatal care affect not only the detection of the virus in mothers and babies, but also in the follow up that identified patients should have.

Boys and girls in Guyana are exposed to elevated levels of sexual, psychological and physical abuse at home and in their communities, as well as child trafficking and child labour. Gender based violence contributes to the aggravated situation of violence against children.

Abuse and violence against women and children are related to the power control that men try to exercise over the women, which is also extended to the children. While legislation to prevent abuse and punish perpetrators exists, the implementation of the different legal norms is still lagging behind. Impunity is seen as a major bottleneck in the system, caused by victims and witnesses that are afraid of reporting abuses – sometimes due to personal or financial connection to the perpetrator.

Despite improvements in the socio-economic situation in the country, inequity is a major factor in Guyana, i.e. boys and girls do not have access to the same quality of education, health and child protection due to the structural problems outlined above.

THE ETHOS OF THE YCMTW PROGRAMME

The goal of the Youth Can Move the World programme was to give youth a forum in which to discuss and analyse social issues, and to get them to reflect on the process of personal and community transformation. We first organised a series of consultations with youth across the country, including remote areas in the interior of Guyana. Youth were invited to these gatherings through notices in schools, community centres and the media. Efforts were made to ensure the groups reflected the diversity of the population. The focus at these consultations was simply to listen to their concerns.

Many of the youth were disillusioned with the prevailing materialistic concept of education which failed to touch their lives in a meaningful way. The challenge of the programme was to awaken youth to an appreciation of the possibilities of their own lives and to foster the development of the full range of their human capacities and to appreciate that education is the key to a just, peaceful and meaningful life.

The YCMTW programme was initially funded by UNICEF as one response to the HIV/AIDs challenge in Guyana. However, UNICEF accepted the adoption of an integrated approach that did not just look at HIV/AIDs but saw the wider issues of domestic violence, illiteracy, poverty and gender inequality. The YCMTW programme helped the youth expand their vision to the possibilities of their own lives and to develop their capacity to think critically and to begin a dialogue with their peers on the type of society they wanted. YCMTW began with simple actions which became more complex thereby increasing the self-confidence, and self-respect of the youth. They were given tools to work with their communities.

Participants in the YCMTW programme

UNICEF sponsorship of YCMTW

Former First Lady, Mrs Uma Jagdeo, at the YCMTW graduation

In the YCMTW programme youth acquire knowledge of social issues, involve themselves in the development of their communities, engage in reflection on their spiritual condition and personal choices. The goal of YCMTW is to raise up a generation of leaders with a feeling of personal responsibility for the advancement of their communities and the wider society.

YCMTW IN ACTION

The focus for the YCMTW programme came out of the discussions with young people. The topics selected for the programme were: protection of the environment, domestic violence, HIV/AIDS, prevention of suicide, human rights, gender equity, global prosperity, and drug and alcohol abuse. The programme adopted a 'trainer of trainers' approach. A 70-hour, training programme was developed for youth between the ages of 16 to 25 years who would then take the programme to their own communities. The goal was to use youth themselves as agents of social change. An integral element of the programme was the use of the arts, in the form of songs, puppets, posters, stories, banners, board games, and pamphlets to communicate the social messages.

The Training Manual was produced in consultation with persons from the Ministry of Health and the Ministry of Education, and a variety of NGOs including those working in the areas of domestic violence, HIV/AIDS, protection of the environment, suicide prevention, rights of the child and gender equity. These same agencies then shared responsibility for the training of the youth volunteers.

The majority of these agencies had considerable experience in training youth. However, there were at least two groups who presented their topics in a 'top-down' rather than in a participatory and interactive fashion. Sessions were therefore held with these personnel to ensure that their training methodology mirrored that adopted by their more experienced NGO colleagues.

GUYANA CHRONICLE Monday, February 3, 2003

Hundreds trained through Varqa Foundation youth leadership scheme

- coordinator

YOUTH Can Move the World programme has trained 900 leaders as facilitators and approximately 1,800 were enlightened through the same training, which started four years ago, one of the coordinators, Ms Shireen Cade reported.

She said the process is geared to equip the beneficiaries with the know-how to deal with burning issues affecting young Guyanese, so they can return to their respective communities and share the knowledge.

Cade told the Chronicle that the initial scheme was implemented in July 1999 and has since coursed five batches, with another graduating this year July.

She said some of the topics covered are HIV/AIDS, domestic violence, drugs and alcohol abuse, suicide, poverty and literacy.

According to Cade, extensive use is made of the arts, in the form of banners, puppetry, songs, dance and drama.

She explained that the first phase involves training at School of the Nations and those trainees return to their different communities to train other youths in the second and final phases.

The current batch of 250 is divided into 50 groups and they are now active in the second phase, training in all ten Administrative Regions of Guyana.

Cade said graduates from the hinterland, who also had the benefit, will be visited and updated by a team from Varqa Foundation.

She disclosed that scholarship support is available from United Nations Children's Fund (UNICEF) for youths from Essequibo, Berbice and Linden to attend courses in Georgetown.

Meanwhile, a year-end festival will highlight their achievements and successful participants will be awarded University of Guyana (UG) certificates.

The project, organised by Varqa, is sponsored by UNICEF, Canadian International Development Agency (CIDA) and the Baha'i community, in collaboration with UG.

One of the beneficiaries, 17-year-old Diana Ross said it is rewarding and she is now teaching 20 other teenagers in Campbellville, Georgetown.

"It is making a difference in their lives. It is having a tremendous impact on my life and it is very educational. I am able to help others who are not in a position to learn about social issues," she commented.

Guyana Chronicle Newspaper, Feb 3rd 2003

UNICEF support

GUYANA CHRONICLE Tuesday, November 5, 2001

A Lodge Truth Centre participant receives the Festival Trophy for her group's song from Dr Sreelakshmi Gururaja, Assistant UNICEF Representative.

154 attend 'Youth Can Move The World' workshop

ONE hundred and fifty-four youths gathered at the School of the Nations on the weekend of October 26-28 to participate in the 'Youth Can Move The World' training workshop.

Through the financial assistance of the United Nations Children's Fund (UNICEF), a total of 22 Amerindian youths were able to attend the workshop, a release from the Varqa Foundation stated.

Minister of Amerindian Affairs, Ms Carolyn Rodrigues and her Adviser, Ms Juliet Solomon made the logistical arrangements, while personnel of Trans Guyana Airways gave invaluable assistance by organising plane tickets for the participants.

The Saturday of the weekend featured the graduation of the second batch of Youth Can Move the World (YCMTW) facilitators. At this event, there were creative presentations from the graduands based on themes explored during previous seminars.

The Lodge Truth Church Youth group, under the guidance of Mrs Barbara Deodat, performed consistently well in all the various categories and won a number of the trophies for first place.

During the weekend seminar, sessions were conducted on 'Suicide Prevention' by Mrs Kala Seegopaul, while the subject of 'Global Prosperity' was dealt with by Dr Brian O'Toole.

Ms Gail Teixeira, Minister of Culture, Youth and Sport, was among persons addressing the gathering of young people.

A second weekend of training is planned for November 16-18 and that workshop will also be held at School of the Nations. Presenters at that seminar will include the First Lady Mrs Varshnie Jagdeo, and personnel from the Help and Shelter agency.

Following the six days of training, the youth facilitators will return to their own communities to take their peers through the same materials. Illustrated facilitators and participants' manuals have been produced and field-tested over the past three years.

A programme is already in place at the Anna Regina Multilateral School, under which, all the teachers are being trained as YCMTW facilitators. Consultations are also in progress with educators in West Coast Berbice to introduce the Youth Can Move The World programme in Region Five.

The Varqa Foundation, which operates YCMTW programme and the 'On the Wings of Words' literacy project, is collaborating with Videomega Productions to create a series of 15-minute video films on YCMTW themes. The YCMTW manual is now in use in Canada and Ethiopia.

YCMTW is funded by UNICEF, the CIDA gender programme and the International Baha'i Community. The programme is operated in conjunction with the Institute of Distance and Continuing Education (IDCE), University of Guyana.

Information on the next training workshop can be obtained from the Varqa Foundation, 120 Parade Street, Kingston; and on telephone numbers: 226-7870, 226-5781 or 621-4615.

A Youth Can Move The World graduate is presented with her certificate by Mr Samuel Small of the Institute of Distance and Continuing Education.

Minister of Culture, Youth and Sport Ms Gail Teixeira addresses the workshop.

The late Mr Sammy Small, Head of IDCE at the University of Guyana, addresses the
YCMTW Graduation. Guyana Chronicle Newspaper, Nov 5th, 2001

An illustrated Animator's Manual was produced for the course with:
- Background information on each of the major topics
- Quotes from the major religions of Guyana on these issues
- Suggestions for practical ways to present each of the topics using the arts

In addition, a Participant's Manual was also produced for the YCMTW facilitators to use in their own communities with youth aged 11 to 14 years. The YCMTW training was advertised in the media inviting persons to participate. Applicants needed a letter of endorsement from a community leader. The YCMTW participants came from a wide range of backgrounds including church groups, youth clubs and schools. When asked why they wanted to be involved in the programme many said they simply wanted "to be of service to their own communities".

The YCMTW programme was offered as a programme from the External Department of the University of Guyana so that participants who attended the 70 hours of training and undertook a minimum of 12 sessions of training in their own community would earn a Certificate from the University of Guyana. The First Lady and the Head of UNICEF attended the first Graduation. The First Lady sent a seven-page letter to the Graduates of the first YCMTW training.

LOCAL TRAINING

Once trained, the youth would then return to their communities and begin a similar training with young people aged 11 to 14 years, on an unpaid voluntary basis. The training was carried out in schools, youth clubs, and religious groups. The YCMTW participants provided invaluable role models to younger persons within their own communities. Sadly, such role models have been in short supply in Guyana.

A team of 17 animators was also recruited and given seven additional days of training. The majority of these animators had already served the programme as volunteers on earlier YCMTW programmes in their regions. They undertook visits to YCMTW groups to accompany the volunteer trainers and help maintain their enthusiasm for the programme. They held 'Look Back and Step Ahead' follow-up meetings every three months where additional training was offered to the leaders to give them the opportunity for an on-going process of monitoring and evaluation. It also helped to maintain the interest of the volunteers in the programme.

Over the 15 years that the YCMTW programme operated, almost 1,000 youth facilitators were trained, who, in turn, worked with more than 7,000 youth in 120 YCMTW groups throughout the country.

THE SPIRITUAL REQUIREMENTS OF LIFE

The YCMTW programme tried to create a coherence between spiritual and practical requirements of life. It also tried to create an integrated model of development as fragmented activities surely do not lead to sustainable development.

An integral part of YCMTW was the undertaking of the Bahá'í inspired, Ruhi spiritual enrichment programme which integrates group study, service and use of the arts. The goal of this aspect of the YCMTW programme was intellectual and spiritual transformation.

The Ruhi materials encourage structured group discussion of passages from the Bahá'í Writings. However, in light of Guyana's multi religious backgrounds the participants were, of course, free to draw on their own religious writings for inspiration. The YCMTW participants accepted that a programme concerned with social transformation should address the spiritual dimension and our own moral purpose and capacity for service.

The YCMTW facilitators then worked with youth aged, 11 to 14 in their own communities. They aimed to engage the interest of their members, moulded their capacity for service, and involved them in social interaction

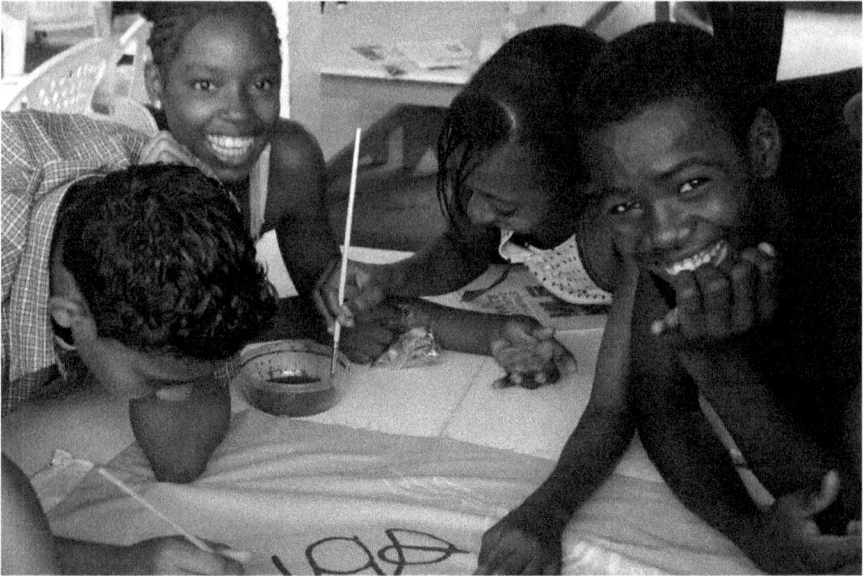

YCMTW training sessions

with older youth. Typical sessions began with prayers, songs and games. The small group study format helped them develop literacy skills to empower the junior youth. After the group study the youth would engage in arts (dance, drama, singing, painting) and then discuss social issues which are featured in the Animator's Manual. A typical session would then close with a period of reflection and sharing what they learned in the day.

DEVELOPMENTS FROM YCMTW

One of the significant achievements of the YCMTW programme was the way in which a core group of YCMTW animators from one interior area of Guyana, the Rupununi, comprised of the indigenous people of the country, received further training to take the programme to two new very isolated Amerindian regions of the country. This was the first time that indigenous persons had been the key facilitators in a programme rather than their customary role of recipient of inputs from others. UNICEF provided funds to facilitate this process for a group of 22 Amerindians to be trained as facilitators. This training was organised in collaboration with the Ministry of Amerindian Affairs and the Regional Education Department of the Rupununi.

In the very isolated community of Kato, in the Pakaraimas, Region #8, a one-week YCMTW workshop was therefore held by their peers from the Rupununi for 32 youth. Two further weekend workshops in the Pakaraimas were held for another 68 youth.   In the Rupununi region, on the border with Brazil, weekly sessions were held at the major Secondary school for 75 youth.   In another interior Amerindian area, Santa Mission, Region #4, a further one-week workshop was held for 52 youth. In Jacklow, in the Pomeroon River, Region #2, weekly sessions were held for 42 youth aged 12 to 16 years and at a prominent school in the capital, 120 youth studied the YCMTW programme each week for a year.

The success of the YCMTW attracted the attention of a wide variety of international agencies. VF was invited by the Inter-American Development

Bank (IADB) to undertake a major study of the impact of HIV/AIDS projects in Guyana. The YCMTW facilitators were also mobilised by UNICEF to undertake a major survey re HIV AIDS in 2003 of 3,500 persons aged 14 to 30 years.

YCMTW was commissioned by UNICEF and the National Commission on the Rights of the Child to produce, in collaboration with the YCMTW facilitators, a series of 60 second videos on 'sport for the development of peace.'

The UNICEF HIV prevention programme that was undertaken by the YCMTW programme in April 2003, trained 250 persons in 7 of the 10 regions of Guyana using 24 YCMTW animators from previous YCMTW training. They met monthly to review the programme, arrange visits to YCMTW groups and to see how to make the programme stronger.

The Health and Family Life (HFLE) programme of the Ministry of Education sought to integrate YCMTW into the national HFLE programme

In October 2004, VF undertook a Child Labour programme in collaboration with the International Labour Organisation (ILO) working with 60 child labourers and 150 children in danger of becoming child labourers. The ILO shared with us that they regarded this programme as their most dynamic of all their programmes in the Caribbean. The programme was therefore extended for a further six months. The intervention focussed on training in sewing, hair dressing, curtain making, and training to become a mechanic. Marches were also organised on the theme of 'World Day Against Child Labour'. VF was given a Culture Grant from IADB to the value of US$5,000. YCMTW attracted extensive media coverage, the American journal, 'One Country' carried an in-depth article on the YCMTW programme in October 2005. Vision TV, from Canada, produced a documentary on the YCMTW programme that was seen by thousands of persons in Canada. Elijah Marchand, a professional videographer from Canada, spent 6 months in Guyana on the YCMTW programme making videos on the intervention.

With the movement away from national to regional trainings ownership of the YCMTW process was transferred to the Regional level. This was consolidated by the creation of regional YCMTW Committees in 6 of the 10 regions of Guyana.

LESSONS LEARNT

In developing the YCMTW programme VF formed effective partnerships with a range of agencies. VF attracted researchers from the University of Edmonton, McMaster University and Queens University to offer their insights on the programme. Karen Brookes undertook an evaluation of YCMTW for her Master's thesis at the University of Michigan.

Volunteers came to assist with the YCMTW programme from Health for Humanity (HH), a Bahá'í inspired health agency. The chapter in this book on the Rupununi has explored this partnership. Over the course of 15 years, Health for Humanity sent a total of 28 health professionals to serve on the VF initiatives, mainly to assist with the trainings. The initial partnership was based on an older model of development in terms of donating equipment for the hospital in the interior. Over the years however a wider perspective emerged by which highly trained health professionals came to join the VF projects for a few weeks to strengthen these initiatives and to be the wind in the sails of others. It should be noted however that not all these professionals were comfortable with this role. Some were more accustomed to roles in the front seats and at the helm of the ship. In future programmes this challenge needs to be addressed to see how to make the most effective use of Western trained 'experts.'

A very effective partnership was the one formed with Nancy Campbell Academy (NCA) and their Wildfire Dance Workshop. That team came to Guyana for a month to raise up a team from the YCMTW participants to introduce the themes from the YCMTW manual in the form of dance and song. In January 2018 NCA sent another team to Guyana.

The issues that the YCMTW programme focussed on emerged out of a series of village meeting that the VF coordinators held throughout one of the interior regions of Guyana. The development of the various aspects of the YCMTW manual was then nurtured in consultation with the key bodies in Guyana working in those areas eg, The Environmental Protection Agency, the National Commission on the Rights of the Child, the Health and Family Life Education Programme, and the Ministry of Health. These consultations helped to present the programme as a unified vision by a number of key agencies and warned away potential critics.

The direct mail out to more than 1,000 persons to advertise the programme and the requirement to have a letter of endorsement from a community leader helped to both popularise the programme and to establish certain standards.

CHALLENGES: WHAT REMAINS OF THE YCMTW PROGRAMME TODAY?

At the outset of the programme there were those who said that the Ruhi materials were too overtly Bahá'í and that this, in the multi religious context of Guyana, might alienate certain sections of the population. As a compromise in the first year we removed the word 'Bahá'í' from all the quotes. But like most compromises this didn't satisfy many. In the second year we included quotes from all the major religions of the country. By the third year however we partnered with the National Institute Board (NIB) of the Bahá'ís of Guyana and they took full responsibility for the Ruhi training part of YCMTW using the original and complete versions of the Ruhi materials.

In practice however, there was very little resistance from the participants to the Ruhi materials. The great majority of the youth embraced the process with interest and enthusiasm and proved to be very committed to the memorisation and service aspects of the training.

One girl had been abandoned by her father at birth and loathed him as a result. However, in Book #1 of the Ruhi materials she learnt, "A thought of hatred must be destroyed by a more powerful thought of love." She therefore found him, forgave him and formed a new relationship with him.

However, there were not enough animators to sustain all the local groups. An intensive training was required, which however never took place, to address this need. As a stop-gap measure a number of Canadian youth volunteered their time to the programme. However, a number of them were ill-prepared for this role. More thought needs to be invested concerning the skills and preparation required of the tutors. How can we best promote and nurture the qualities of persistence, flexibility, and encouragement as they refine the art of accompaniment?

Also, in retrospect it was a mistake to present the YCMTW programme as a '12-month intervention' as it suggested to the participants that after one year they would move on to other things.

UNICEF was unable to endorse the spiritual component in keeping with their mandate; unhappy in having the spiritual component endorsed by them. We were fortunate therefore that the International Bahá'í Community quickly stepped in to fund this aspect of the programme. Two manuals were then produced, one sponsored by UNICEF, focussing on the social issues and the use of the arts, and the other, sponsored by the Bahá'í community, which focussed on the Ruhi materials.

We hear daily that we live in a new age and that we are now a global society. Education needs to prepare persons for the new world order and excite them with new possibilities and present them with a new reality.

The YCMTW programme therefore responded to the present and future needs of Guyanese adolescents and young adults. It provided a forum for youth to express themselves on issues that affected them daily. The programme effectively raised up a cadre of youth to be of service to their peers. It demonstrated how youth can serve as facilitators of a programme of this nature. It also gave youth a forum to reflect on the spiritual foundation to social issues.

However, the YCMTW programme as such no longer exists. Some of the greatest resistance to this exciting programme came from sections of our own faith community who felt that our efforts might have been invested more productively in other endeavours. In response we now introduce elements of the YCMTW programme into the various service programmes that we offer out of School of Nations.

The contribution below from the two youth who served as the coordinators of the YCMTW programme, Rosheni Takechandra and Lomeharshan Lall, outline what they feel were the key aspects of the intervention.

REFLECTION *by Rosheni Takechandra*

The year was 2005. I had just graduated from high school. A friend showed me the Youth Can Move the World advert in the newspaper. Coming from a conservative family where girls are not allowed to sleep away from home, it was the first time I was allowed to be away from home for one month with absolute strangers at the School of Nations - an institution my parents knew little about, and participating in a programme they had never heard about. It was this programme that would later lead me to make the most important decision one could make in their earthly life- the decision to strive by day and by night to apply the Teachings of Bahá'u'lláh to one's life and to strive to be a Bahá'í.

As a participant of the YCMTW programme I was given the opportunity to develop my power of expression, to foster bonds of friendship with persons from various backgrounds and beliefs and to learn to work in small groups to serve my community. The programme gifted me with tools -the Ruhi Institute Courses, the use of the arts to communicate important messages and training to serve as a facilitator - to return to my village and be a youth leader, to hold groups and classes for youth, junior youth and children. It was the fulfilment of my heart's desire.

My life was completely transformed I like to say. Now I realise that transformation is a process but at that time I felt like it was the best I've felt in my life.. I found purpose - a purpose that was shaped by the Teachings of Bahá'u'lláh. Undesirable behaviours and attitudes were gradually fading. A new mindset emerged and was fostered - one that encompassed the oneness of mankind and the oneness of God. It was this programme that made me want to find my talent and develop it, that I might be able to serve humanity in greater capacity. It gave me a high sense of purpose in my little life.

By the time I was eighteen years old, I started to serve as the national YCMTW coordinator. It was during this time that I witnessed the transformative energy that is released when engaging a large number of youth in the community-building process. I saw how believing and trusting in the capacities of young people to be agents of change was translated into their empowerment, how the power to effect change and transformation is greater when there is collaboration and cooperation among like-minded groups, how consultation can resolve challenges and find solutions that foster unity and how supporting structures can emerge to support grassroots action. This foundation for community building has been instrumental in my professional and spiritual development. It makes me see opportunities in every neighbourhood, village, town and country.

Today every decision I make in my professional life is shaped by my love for using spiritual principles for social good and for economic development. Every decision I make in my personal life is guided by the Teachings of the Bahá'í Faith — a Faith I was oblivious to prior to the YCMTW programme.

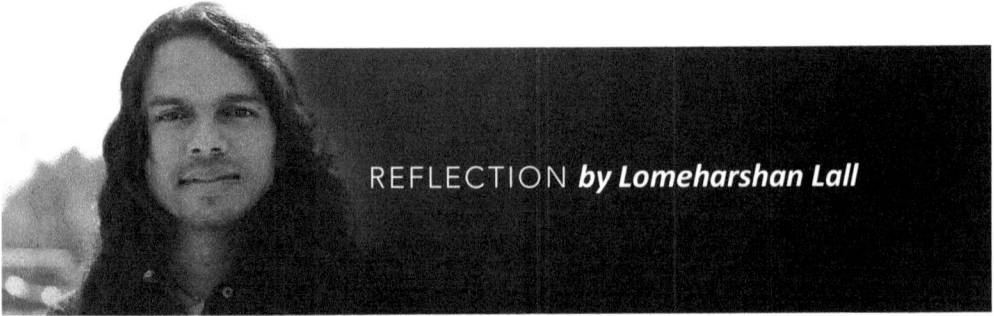

REFLECTION *by Lomeharshan Lall*

The design of the YCMTW programme was able to tap into the inherent desire of the youth of Guyana to contribute to the betterment of their communities. Youth from every cross section of society were attracted and the programme was designed to facilitate large numbers.

I was one of the youth who responded to the newspaper advert re YCMTW. The programme drastically changed my life. Coming from one of the worst places to live in Guyana with oppressive poverty, violence and substance abuse, my fate was projected to reflect the lifestyle of the people in my neighbourhood. The programme however instilled a strong sense of hope, encouraging me to open my eyes to the possibility of contributing to the betterment of the world by helping my community combat the myriad social ills the youth face. The structure of the programme gave me the skills, attitudes, knowledge and capacity to not only contribute to my growth but to that of others. One of the most important and core beliefs of the programme is the Vision of Bahá'u'lláh of the oneness of humanity. When I heard this I instantly realized what else is there to spend my life to promote. This value governs every aspect of my life now - family, friends, school, work, etc.

The programme also facilitated my growth in offering me opportunities to serve in more complex ways. I started facilitating trainings at the programme and soon served as a coordinator for the programme. This built my capacity to think about community building in a systematic way.

Ruhi training session at YCMTW

Steps towards a new model of Educational Leadership: Lessons from School of Nations in Guyana

Brian O'Toole

INTRODUCTION

It was 1996 and I was in Ghana undertaking a UNICEF consultancy. The weekend was free so my friend invited me to Togoland to visit a school run by a young Bahá'í couple. The school proved to be an oasis of peace set amidst a troubled capital. The visit was all the more timely as my two boys were then attending one of the leading government schools in Guyana. However, each evening, over dinner, they would tell me that two, three or even four of the teachers did not turn up to teach their class that day. When I visited the school the Head Teacher told me, "don't worry we should be getting a Maths teacher sometime next year."

The visit to the school in Togoland was in April, by August we were ready to open School of Nations in Guyana. This chapter traces the evolution and development of the last twenty years of School of Nations. Nations represents our attempt to put the fine sounding principles of the Bahá'í Faith into practice in terms of creating a different model of education.

EDUCATION INDICATORS IN GUYANA

Number of schools in Guyana:	
113	Nursery schools
148	Primary schools
82	Secondary schools
58	Private schools
7	Special schools or units
4	Technical Institutes
1	School of Home Economics
1	Teacher Training College
1	Government University

The average salary of trained teachers is in the region of US$500 (net) per month and for an untrained teacher about US$250 (net) per month.

School attendance:
94,000 in Primary schools
56,000 in Lower Secondary (ie 12 to 14 years)
30,000 in Upper Secondary (ie 15 to 16 years)

Ref: https://www.epdc.org

LITERACY LEVEL:

The literacy level quoted by www.epdc.org is 93%, as defined by; the ability to read and write with understanding a simple statement related to one's daily life. NB This figure is seriously challenged in this book in the chapter 'On the Wings of Words.'

TEACHER TRAINING:

Lilian Dewar Teacher Training College was founded in 1968 to train secondary teachers. (The author of this book worked there for three years from 1978 to 1981)

Making a start on renovating and building School of Nations

Cyril Potter College of Education offers a two-year training programme for primary teachers and a three-year training for secondary and vocational teachers. The entrance qualification to enter the College is 4 CSEC and OL (these are the exams student sit at 15 and 16 years of age) subjects including English and Mathematics.

Between 1995 to 2000 a total of 2,200 persons were trained at the Teacher Training College.

The University of Guyana (the only government University in Guyana) offers Diploma, Bachelor's and Master's Degrees in Education. It is said that 85% of the graduates leave each year for jobs overseas.

Renovating and building School of Nations

GUYANA EDUCATION SECTOR PLAN 2014 TO 2018

This plan was based on a wide consultation with a variety of stakeholders. They stated the desire to, "work out decreasing the differences in the learning outcomes between students in coastal and hinterland schools .... Learning outcomes of primary concern are literacy and numeracy followed by science and technology" and the Plan expressed a "concern for at risk and vulnerable children and special needs children."

NEED FOR A NEW MODEL OF EDUCATION

The first line of one of John Holt's books states, "most children in school fail." (Holt,1964). They fail to develop more than a tiny part of their potential. Schools, not just in Guyana but, throughout the world rob children of their youth, their creativity and their self-respect. They are robbed of their youth by having to attend lessons before and after school, they are deprived of their creativity by being regarded as empty vessels to be filled with information and they are robbed of their self-respect by being constantly lectured.

As Paulo Freire (2000) says, children at school are simply like tellers in a bank. Their mission is to receive, file and store the deposits made by their teachers. This results in passive, bored, frustrated and dependent learners. As always, it is easier to criticise than to offer meaningful alternatives. But a new model of education sees children as storehouses of intellectual, artistic, moral, emotional and spiritual potential. The teacher's role then becomes an awakener of the learner, to challenge the child to think, to be productive, to consult and to listen to others and to begin to investigate for him/herself.

Children then move from being spectators to being actors, from being the objects of learning to being the key actors in the process. We therefore need a re-definition of what education is. The task of education therefore becomes the release of the child's potential by providing the necessary

The opening of the new buildings for Nations by, the then, Prime Minister Mr. Sam Hinds

School of Nations branch in Berbice

environmental conditions, resources and actions to facilitate that growth. Yet internationally the task of education is submerged beneath test scores, an obsession with numbers leading to a loss of the magic and mystery of teaching. By only focussing on test- driven goals teachers have no time to reflect on the art of teaching. The danger is that we look only at what is easy to measure.

There needs to be a new-found recognition that good teaching is in fact very difficult and needs considerable investment in training and constant practice. Essential to a re-definition of education is the need for time for reflection on the part of teachers. They need to challenge the status quo and not be fearful of admitting their own vulnerabilities. We need to help teachers to have frank and productive conversations and move them beyond their comfort zones. Teachers need to learn how to collaborate with others.

At School of Nations we have tried to promote some of the capabilities as outlined by Nur University (Anello, 2001)

- Being able to evaluate one's strengths and weaknesses without becoming egotistical or defensive
- To think systematically in search of solutions

- To imbue our thoughts and actions with love
- To encourage others and bring joy to their hearts
- To build unity in diversity
- To persevere and overcome obstacles
- To oppose lower passions by focussing on higher purposes
- To foster a love of learning
- To realize that human happiness lies in spiritual and intellectual development and not via wealth and power
- To appreciate that the earth is but one country and mankind its citizens

The task of education then becomes to:

- Awaken the child's natural capacity for intellectual investigation
- Promote an understanding of the natural world
- Develop proficiency in at least one productive skill
- Analyse social conditions and discover the forces which influence them
- Understand the need for programmes of social betterment in health, sanitation, agriculture and crafts

The goal is to build a new global society. Our task is to nurture youth to be scientifically, musically, artistically literate and to create a morally inspired education which unites human, material and spiritual values. In turn, children will become active, responsible learners who are architects of their own growth. Schools which are inspired with such values promote world awareness, champion diversity, inspire a spirit of co-operation and service, promote a profound care for others, develop strength to meet life's challenges and enkindle a fundamental desire to excel.

PIONEERING A NEW FORM OF EDUCATION

In Guyana we have been given the opportunity to translate these fine sounding principles into action. We see our role as 'nurturing the gems'. Our task is to promote the knowledge, qualities, skills and attitudes that would contribute to building a New World Order.

We started SON in the capital in 1996. It now has a pre-school, nursery, primary, secondary, special unit and a University. SON has 825 students, 80 teachers and 48 other staff. The tertiary part of Nations now has more than 2,200 students.

The curriculum at Nations up to Form 3 follows that supplied by the Ministry of Education for schools in Guyana. In Form 3 the students begin to focus on preparation for their IGCSE examinations from Cambridge International Examinations from the University of Cambridge. In the 4th and 5th Forms the students sit the Cambridge IGCSE examinations and in Lower and Upper Sixth Form they take Cambridge Advance Subsidiary and Advanced Level examinations. Plans are also in train to earn accreditation for Nations as a US High School.

Timeline of the growth of School of Nations (SON):
• June 1996: SON rents premises and 'enrols' its first 5 students
• Sept. 1996: SON opens with 186 students from Nursery to 3rd Form
• Over the years the following persons have served as Principal; Christine Brisport, Pamela O'Toole, Gloria Nandan, Orin Ross and Mischka White
• Sept. 1997 opening of the Sixth Form
• 2001: Special Needs Unit opened
• 2004: School of Nations pro-bono branch opened in New Amsterdam (70 miles from the capital)
• Sept. 2012 Nations purchases its own building
• Jan. 2018: (including the University) Nations is a community of more than 3,000 students representing 42 countries. The 'overseas' students are from foreigners working in Guyana. They represent about 15% of the school population

After starting SON however, it did not take us long to appreciate what a demanding journey this would be. We were at once expected to address special needs, social work issues, behaviour and social problems, and unrealistic parents' and administrator's expectations. We began to wonder how it would be possible to manage so many challenges.

Locally recruited teachers entered Nations from the jaundiced experience of large class sizes, great ranges of ability within a single class, very different learning styles, limited investment in professional development, outside appraisals of a punitive nature, and teachers being perceived as a large part of the problem in education, rather than as the key to the solution. For many of them the pleasure had been taken out of teaching. Our task at Nations was to see if we could re build professional capital back into their roles.

But we very soon realised this would be no easy task to change the teachers' understanding of the role of teachers and education. Our task was to conceive teaching as a collaborative undertaking. Was it possible to attract more qualified teachers to Nations? What types of teachers should we be looking for? Could we at SON begin to develop a more professional role for teachers? Could more rigorous training, with on-going in-service training, begin to develop a more professional role for the teacher?

In helping to articulate a new model of education we benefited from insights from Hargreaves and Fullan (2012). They note how in countries like Finland, Singapore, Canada and South Korea there are very few private schools, and teachers are drawn from the top graduates in the country. In these countries teaching is a very attractive profession. In Singapore, for example, the starting salary for teachers compares favourably with that of engineers. In Finland teachers spend less time in classrooms than any other developed country. This leaves them time to reflect on what they are doing, to become more creative, and contribute to the social prosperity of the country. In USA, by comparison, education is more a task of competition rather than collaboration, often teaching is not seen as an attractive profession, it is an individual rather than a collective enterprise.

In developing this new approach we were mindful that we needed to adopt a model of education based on 'leadership' as opposed to 'management'. We needed to explore what practical skills therefore needed to be developed and how to foster a climate in which transformational leadership would be nurtured. We needed to understand what such a model would look like. This was all the more urgent in that the Ministry of Education had earlier stated, "the Secondary education system in Guyana, like the Primary is in a state of near collapse."

Could a new vision of teachers and education be created within such a pessimistic environment? What innovations would be required to create that new model? On-going training would be at the heart of this venture, along with continuous practice and the need to see the challenge as a collective enterprise. We should be challenged to see how to continuously improve our own teaching and understand the art and craft of teaching better. We need to get back some of the magic of teaching.

One of the guiding principle for Nations from the inception was the quote from Bahá'u'lláh the Prophet Founder of the Bahá'í Faith:

"Regard man as a mine rich in gems of inestimable value, education can alone cause it to reveal its treasures and enable mankind to benefit therefrom."

Guyana has many mines. We had visited some of the gold mines and had seen the ugliness of the raw gold that miners sacrificed so much to unearth. But they persevered in their efforts because of the reward at the end. It would surely be the same in education. Somehow, we needed to share the belief with our teachers that those hidden gems were there to be discovered, but just as with the miners, it would take great effort to discover.

Hargreaves & Fullan (2012) emphasise the need for far more professionalism in teaching and education and to examine what is the key to transforming any culture. Professionals are expected to be impartial, to uphold high standards of conduct, to display specialised knowledge and then they should be given the status and rewards comparable to other professions.

We need to get teachers to move away from their isolation and work in teams and focus on transforming the whole school. New patters of communication within schools need to be established along with the establishment of new relationships. Teachers will not admit to problems if they think it will affect their performance appraisals. They need to have access to new ideas and remove the fear of changing the institutionalised conservatism in our schools.

Schools foster isolation to avoid scrutiny. Guilt and frustration plague our teachers. By contrast the few teachers that come from a collaborative culture are very different. They welcome the role of challenging the status quo. They are not plagued by the fear of failure rather these challenges are discussed openly. In such an environment open discussion and temporary disagreements will not threaten existing relationships. In such schools, teachers work in groups engaged in frank and productive conversations. Teachers should be encouraged to venture out from their comfort zones.

But in our experience precious few teachers had travelled this route before coming to Nations. Also, one needs to consider whether the scenarios presented by Hargreaves and Fullan (2012) are easier in the context of

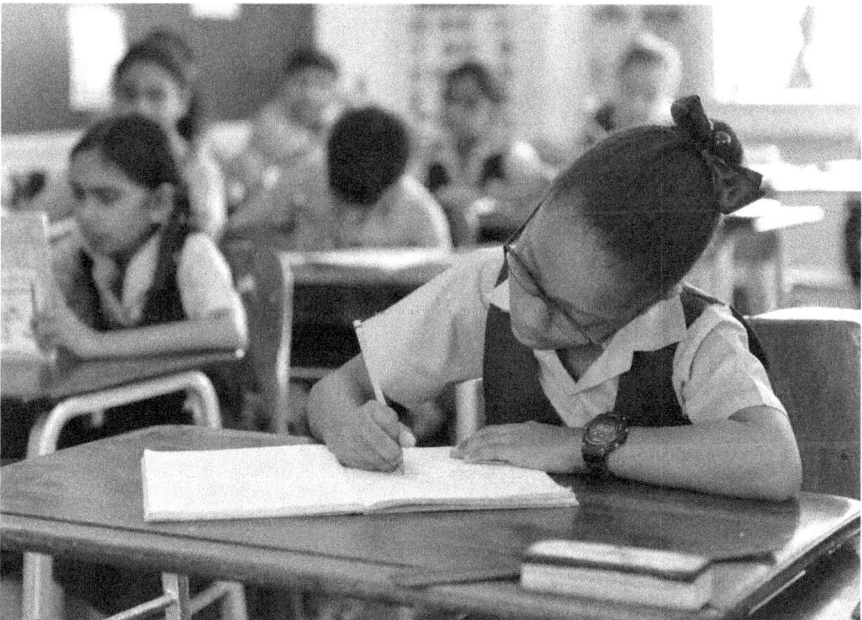

Asian culture. In such cultures there is a greater tradition of historical respect for the teacher, high family focus on the value of education and clear and established reverence for hierarchies of authority. In such a culture teaching is regarded as a shared purpose, a collective undertaking. How can we therefore develop social capital? We need to appreciate that behaviour is shaped more by the group than the individual.

SOME OF THE KEY LESSONS WE LEARNT INCLUDED;

DEVELOP A VISION

Many years ago, Ghandi issued the admonition, "be the change you want to see". The challenge was therefore ours to map out a vision for Nations. Our task was to try and develop a group to envision the change and to believe such innovations could happen. But this takes time and needs a strong foundation at the outset. We realised that we needed to raise the bar to what teachers expected of themselves, we needed to develop partnerships and replace polarization with integration. We had to move away from the prevailing professional culture of isolation and protectionism and replace distance with integration. Our goal was to help teachers be the best they can be. So, in developing this vision for a new model of education, extensive use was made of in-service training to help the staff reflect on what was required of them.

My wife and I tried to reflect on our own strengths and weaknesses and seek out different perspectives. We were reminded that Walt Disney, in selecting new staff, would always look for persons with very different opinions to his own. We also realised that we could not make demands of persons we didn't know. Our goal was to build a team and move away from the prevailing model of 'separate silos'. There would need to be open communication. We tried to encourage feedback on our own practice and to give and receive feedback as much as we could. We began to reflect on how to bring out the best in others. From the beginning we always worked with the entire staff at Nations and not just the teachers. We reflected on how we could show a commitment to quality teaching and how we could develop professionalism at Nations. We needed to provide coaching and mentoring for the staff and grants for study, internships, and exchanges. We needed to support teachers in their interpersonal problems and, of course, pay teachers properly!

In reforming education Hargreaves and Fullan (2012) emphasise the importance of a sense of national direction as demonstrated in Singapore and South Korea. This is sorely missing in Guyana and made our task far more difficult. Creating a new role for teachers, to encompass social justice and global prosperity, and seeing teachers as nation builders was a major change in thinking.

Many of the most exciting developments at Nations have however emerged in the last year or two. They have been created as a direct result of the foundation that has been established over two decades.

The leadership provided by each of the five persons who served as the Principal of Nations over the 20 years was crucial. Each of them tried to provide an example of effective leadership that inspired change. The vision they developed impacted the whole staff. In looking for new workers, they sought out persons with the necessary qualities to bring about fundamental change.

A major challenge now, as in any innovation, is that of succession. A chance meeting in New York led us to consulting with Dr. Dexter Phillips and Mrs Simone Phillips. Both Dexter and Simone had worked at Nations in the early days. They then left Guyana to pursue distinguished careers in international schools in China, the Middle East and the Philippines. Dexter earned his PhD, MBA and wrote a widely recognised textbook for Business students. Simone earned her Masters in Educational Leadership. When we met they were working at a US$50,000 a year New York High School for Chinese students. But, thankfully ... they wanted to return to their home, to Guyana. Dexter has accepted the position as the Chief Executive Officer at Nations and Simone is to play a key teaching and admin role. Pam and I, and Liam and Cairan, our sons and fellow Directors, are very confident the school will therefore be in outstanding hands as we transition to new areas of operation and management.

FAITH AND TRUST IN THE PEOPLE WE WERE WORKING WITH

Throughout this journey we have tried to maintain a high level of faith in those with whom we work and the belief that the potential exists within the pool of teachers at our disposal to bring about fundamental change. We also learnt that we needed to delegate and continue to trust where others may have pursued a more unilateral approach

It is not unusual for a 6th Form College to form a Student Council. What was perhaps rather more remarkable at Nations was the fact that the newly elected 6th Form Council took on the government – and won! In 2017 the Government of Guyana decided to implement a 14% VAT on all private education. Within 6 weeks of that announcement the 6th Form Council had gathered more than 15,000 signatures (more than 2% of the entire population) to a petition calling for a recall of that legislation. They wrote letters to the press, appeared on radio and TV programmes and were at the forefront of the movement against the tax. I was contacted by close family urging me not to champion this cause because of the enemies this might attract for Nations. But that is precisely the problem with empowerment: you challenge people to stand up for their rights and you cannot then disassociate yourself from the focus such a movement adopts even if it makes you unpopular in certain political quarters. In December the government repealed the law. Leading commentators in the media attributed the victory to the 6th Form Council, and its 17 and 18-year olds, at Nations.

(See Text box at the end of the chapter)

DEVELOPMENT TAKES TIME

Hargreaves and Fullan (2012,151) state, 'if you want to get big things done get the group to do it.' But, we need to appreciate that it takes time. We need to raise the bar in terms of what should be expected of our co-workers. Obstacles are expected, but they should inspire determination rather than inflicting defeat. For teachers to become true professionals needs perhaps

10,000 hours of research, enquiry and reflection on new ideas. Just as Roger Federer or Christian Ronaldo keep practicing their sports, so too do we need to constantly practice and refine our art as teachers.

INTEGRATED DEVELOPMENT

Throughout this book a theme has emerged that fragmented activities do not produce sustainable development. We need an integrated model of development. Few of the innovations outlined in these chapters would have been possible if we had not already secured a strong academic base at Nations. We have tried to develop an integrated model of development by forging strong partnerships with like-minded agencies.

One example of this is an exciting initiative with the 100 Million Healthier Lives Programme (www.100mlives.org). Dr. Somava Stout, Vice President at the Institute for Healthcare Improvement and Executive Lead of 100 Million Healthier Lives, has visited Guyana on multiple occasions over 20 years to assist with almost all of the development initiatives outlined in this book. She has helped to arrange a partnership for Nations with schools in Wisconsin and Afghanistan that have truly enriched the concept of World Citizenship with our 12th graders. Together, they are developing a curriculum and practicum for service education that trains change makers to know how to be effective in making a difference in the world. By learning to reflect and consult, to lead together with the people most affected by a problem, by using improvement science to learn whether an intervention is truly having an impact, by building collaborations to achieve audacious aims, these youth are developing skills and applying them to improve the lives of the communities around the world.

This world vision has been further expanded by an emerging partnership with the visionary NGO in The Gambia, called Starfish (www.Starfish) which works with more than 100 rural girls to provide them with a broader education and a belief that their surroundings need not constrain their vision of who and what they could become. At Starfish they have clearly demonstrated the need to awaken children to an appreciation of the possibilities of their own lives, to foster the development of the full range of their human capacities and to appreciate that education is the key to a just, peaceful and meaningful life.

Another example of an effective partnership is with Nancy Campbell Academy (NAC) in Canada (http://nancycampbell.ca) NAC was rated #1 school in the whole of Ontario in 2010. They sent two teams of 15 plus students to Nations for a month at a time to train Nations' students in their dance workshop and to help develop the concept of World Citizenship at Nations. As of writing this chapter another team came to Nations for two weeks.

One of the major areas of focus at Nations is the promotion of entrepreneurship training for school leavers through the ABE programme in UK. Training people for jobs in not the focus as there are simply very few jobs available within the Guyana economy at the moment. Rather the training is how to start small businesses. Following a period of training the youth are encouraged to develop a simple business plan which is then presented to funding agencies. This may develop into one of the most important initiatives by Nations. At the end of the day change will only come about for those from humbler backgrounds if they can move away from poverty by creating wealth.

FOCUS ON SERVICE AS AN INTEGRAL PART OF THE SCHOOL EXPERIENCE

An essential feature of Nations is the prominence given to the service programme that all students in the 5th and 6th Forms need to undertake.

For the first 12 years we rented premises for the school. In 2008 we found an ideal location for purchase, but the problem was that it bordered a section of the capital that was known for crime. A number of parents called to say that if we moved to the new location they would remove their children. Undeterred, we bought the property and they stayed with the school. For the past seven years, more than 100 children and youth from the impoverished neighbouring community have come into Nations two or three afternoons per week for free classes, provided by the 6th Formers, in art, music, computers and literacy.   Soon after the move, as if on cue, Nations was robbed of certain equipment and the next thing we saw was the bandits being marched back to Nations, carting the stolen goods and surrounded by the youths from the area.

Recently a prominent NGO in Guyana, 'Epic', invited us to visit a Detention Centre that they are working with. This comprises 30 youth, aged 10 to 16, who have fallen foul of the law and are awaiting trial. The conditions they were housed in was very basic. The 6th Formers now visit the Centre on a daily basis offering mentorship and support in Reading, Math and Computer Studies.

The Interact Club has a membership of more than 100 students from Forms 1-6. Members engage in leadership, project management and many other training activities. They also have a monthly 'meals on wheels' programme where they feed 100 homeless people. The club works with the Police A Division and helps to provide school supplies and Christmas gifts for the 1000 underprivileged children in the division. The club won a National Award for youth volunteerism.

PRO BONO WORK

As stated at the beginning of this book, my wife and I left Britain 40 years ago to try and be of service to the Bahá'í community. The goal, at that time, was not to build a prestigious private school in the capital. Few persons are aware that more than 45 of the students at School of Nations in the capital are on some form of scholarship. The perception of Nations was, and probably still is, that it is the home to children of privilege. Such perceptions are fuelled by the sight of large SUVs in the car park before and after school. The sight of persons walking to school or coming on bicycle is usually overlooked.

In 2008 we started a pro bono branch of Nations in a town, 70 miles from the capital. There are presently 150 children at the school. The school has survived up to now through scholarship support that we have secured from friends in North America and Europe. The goal now is for the school to be totally self-sufficient and we are exploring the introduction of University level courses to this rural school to allow the school to exist independently. In the last year we have been approached by the senior administrators of another major town who have invited Nations to establish a branch in their town using facilities owned by the community.   Nations is also exploring the possibility of starting a centre in Lethem, a town on the border with Brazil. Also in a bid to widen the reach of Nations across the country, six of the AS and AL courses are now available purely as a Distance Education model.

ACADEMIC EXCELLENCE

None of the innovations could however have been introduced unless a strong tradition of academic excellence was established at Nations. If we examine the Cambridge IGCSE and AS/AL examination results for any single year we will see that, on average, 28% of all exams written earned a Grade A or B.

An exciting development this year has been the introduction of the AICE Diploma from Cambridge whereby students have the option to move away from narrow specialisations and adopt more of an International Baccalaurate approach to 6th Form whereby they choose subjects from a far wider range than previously. Furthermore, a new 6th form subject, 'Global Perspectives' has attracted considerable interest. In this course students are encouraged to research, problem solve and explore possible solutions to real issues in their communities. Part of the assessment entails the students filming their final presentations. This, in turn, has helped Nations create its own, professionally equipped, TV studio.

Cambridge International Examinations has recently approached Nations to see if we would be willing to become a Cambridge Associate School and assume responsibility for the whole of the Caribbean to represent and promote Cambridge in the region.

SPECIAL NEEDS

Both my wife and I are trained in the area of Special Needs. Nations has provided a Special Unit for children whose disability is too severe for them to cope within the regular class. In addition, 23 children with special needs have been fully integrated into the main school.

One of our parents introduced us to the Learning Rx programme that he encountered in USA. He paid the US$10,000 franchise fee for Nations to offer the programme in Guyana and we sent three teachers to Denver for intensive training in the methodology. Students from within Nations and outside of Nations are now taking advantage of this new approach to training. Interestingly, this programme is beginning to embrace a far broader definition of "special needs" to include the gifted who are also benefitting significantly from the Brain Rx programme.

WHAT IS SUCCESS IN TERMS OF EDUCATIONAL LEADERSHIP?

We hear daily that we live in a new age. It is a global society. The goals of education and development need to prepare students for this New World Order. We need to excite them with new possibilities and present them with a new reality. Our teachers need to become the new nation builders. We see daily in the news in USA and UK the growing disparity between the haves and the have nots. In recent times this drama has been played out on the streets on both sides of the Atlantic in the form of riots.

This has been an age of slogans, declarations, and conferences in the best hotels, but the danger is that the vast majority of the children in the world remain totally ignorant of the international concern that is being voiced on their behalf. Hence the need for a new model of Educational Leadership.

REFLECTION *by Dr. Dexter Phillips:*
A New Model of Educational Leadership

The literature about Educational Leadership in Guyana is scarce, and, as a result, there are very few credible references that can give a snapshot of the state of leadership in Guyanese schools. In a book chapter entitled, "From Management to Leadership: The case for reforming the practice of secondary education in Guyana," Beepat (2013) advocated for a stronger emphasis on improving leadership practices in Guyana's high schools. He noted that policymakers within the Ministry of Education focus on how well Principals manage, rather than lead, their respective schools.

Leadership refers to Principals' ability to enable, influence, inspire and motivate members of their school communities to contribute towards successful school outcomes. On the other hand, managing schools are about planning, organizing and controlling activities and people to accomplish the desired outcome. Leadership and management are different, yet in practice, complementary. However, too much focus on one aspect is likely to cause more problems than it solves. School Principals, in particular, must lead, and the task of management distributed to ancillary administrators under their direction.

Except for the Certificate in Educational Leadership from Cambridge University offered by Nations School of Education, the education management courses offered through the University of Guyana and the National Centre for Education Resource Development (NCERD), in many respects; back up Beepat's claims. Even though there are snippets of leadership training offered by these institutions, most courses focus heavily on the 'hard' skills required for managing infrastructure, behaviors, and resources; and neglect many of the 'soft' skills necessary for successful leadership of educational institutions.

Further, while the education improvement initiatives outlined in the Ministry of Education's Educational Sector Plan for 2014-2018 are commendable; they lack adequate provision for leadership training of Principals and teachers. Principals need to inspire staff in their schools, so leadership— not management—should drive teaching and learning. In theory and practice, Principals who learn to lead effectively see their schools improve for the long term.

Good Principals, in consort with Heads of Departments and teachers, work purposefully to follow state mandates, enact policies, create clear goals, influence pedagogical practices and student improvement, and build sustainable community relations. They also understand and are aware of changes in the macro and microenvironments that surround their schools, and make decisions based on what is best for protecting and improving students' wellbeing.

Traditionally, school leadership is framed by the transformative contingencies of Principals who can influence behaviors, attitudes and performances. Principals are regarded as a 'solo act' in schools they lead, and do very little to recognize the capacity and potential for shared leadership. This leader-follower model defined school leadership throughout the 19th and 20th centuries. However, over the last decade, organizations have been changing from hierarchical structures to flatter forms and work relationships are based on teams and networks. Individual capabilities, competence and influence in leadership are less important, and there is more focus on the collective efficacy of formal and informal leaders. This is the underlying principle of distributed leadership. This is the new model of leadership, which must be advocated in theory and practice in Guyanese schools.

REFLECTION *by Dr. Ian McDonald*

My wife and I are Catholics. We knew Brian and Pam are Bahá'ís. The difference was bound to be a factor as they explained the concept and the vision of School of Nations twenty-two years ago. The difference was easily accommodated in the concept and the vision. We enrolled our elder son in the new School and later enrolled our younger son. We are pleased to have played a small pioneering role in a huge educational success which has been and is of great and increasing benefit to Guyana.

We have admired and even viewed with wonder as School of Nations has grown from a few junior classes and a handful of students into an organization of more than 3,000 in pre-school, nursery, primary, secondary (including a 6th form of 160 students) and special needs classes and beyond that into a rapidly expanding University system.

It continues to grow while maintaining quality and international standards. It plans to open new branches, reach out further to those with special needs, start a technical training unit, increase the number of scholarships it offers and continually add University courses to its already wide range. Its lasting and growing impact for good on education in Guyana in a difficult time is very important and very valuable.

When School of Nations began I was struck by its founders' awareness that education was not just about cramming facts into students, teaching standardized and memorisable information, getting good examination results at the expense of opening and expanding young minds. Education is really about equipping a child, all children, for the complicated, eternally changing, infinitely challenging world he or she will inherit. There were many other things but Nations it seemed to me stood for that mind and character expanding view of education. I hope it still does and always will.

President of the Student Council at Nations

In 2017 the Guyana government imposed a 14% Value Added Tax on tuition fees at private schools. This new tax would prove to be problematic for all working class parents sending their children to private institutions and for all young adults self-funding their tertiary education. School of Nation's ABE programme had over 100 drop outs as a direct result of this policy. Unfortunately, it was the false perception that schools like School of Nations are attended just by the rich that led to persons saying "if you can afford to send your child to private school then you can afford to pay the tax". Some students may come to Nations in BMWs whilst many others come on bicycles. Private schools are just as diverse as public ones; students come from both humble and blessed backgrounds, all under one roof for one purpose.

The debate on this new tax was spearheaded by the Student Council at Nations. It started with the letters to the editor of daily newspapers written by students from Nations and Dr. Brian O'Toole. This was followed by the creation of an online petition which came out of a Nations' Student Council meeting. We were a small group of students looking to make a change. Together, with the help of the student body we developed a campaign, the epicenter of which was radio and television interviews, letters to the editor, a petition, campaigns at the Giftland Mall, peaceful protest and a meeting with government officials. The petition was signed by more than 15,000 persons in Guyana and by members of the vast Guyanese diaspora in the Americas and Europe. They represented persons of all backgrounds who were brave enough to declare publicly that they disagreed with this policy. This was 2% of the country's population. In January 2018, VAT on private education was finally removed.

REFLECTION *by Mischka White:*
Primary Education in Guyana

Education in Guyana in 2018 unfortunately is still largely an old rigid system of fear, in and during the learning experience as parents, schools and society place excessive pressure on children. The overriding goal is to secure a spot in the top 100, or preferably the top 10 at the National Grade Six Assessment or to gain 16 subjects (or more) in the exams in the secondary. This reduces the learning experience to one of memorization and cramming.

Primary education must focus on mastery of mathematics, reading and comprehension skills that are vital for higher education while also developing the soft skills of compassion, service, tact and equity to empower children to make positive changes in their lives, families and communities.

My experience at School of Nations after working in public education for years is amazing. The classroom for our pupils and students is a safe zone and is centered on exploration, discussion, experimentation and investigative rigour all geared to discovery.

Teachers have a relationship with their pupils and lessons are developed with them in mind. Thus teachers engage their pupils/students and lessons become fun and interactive while learning is occurring in real time as the experiences of our children form the baseline of discussion. Abstract teaching does not ignite the passion for learning and the goal is to make our pupils independent learners.

Art, music, drama are vital elements in the learning equation. Unfortunately, these subjects are largely neglected in the education system in Guyana. Pupils are therefore deprived and potential unrealised. This has led to cultural erosion in our society over many years.

Primary education therefore must be the base for skill and cultural development and should not be tied solely to examinations. School of Nations offers some pathways to follow.

Scenes from School of Nations in Georgetown

CHAPTER 6

Nations University:
Widening Access to Higher Education

Brian O'Toole

INTRODUCTION

A few months ago, a young Guyanese lady came into my office. It was the first time we had met. She began talking with a deep New York accent and said she wanted to thank me because we had saved her at least US$50,000 as she was just about to pursue an MBA in New York when she came across our MBA programme at Nations University at less than US$7,700. Now other Guyanese from the diaspora in New York and Toronto are doing the same.

Pam and I arrived in Guyana many years ago after taking full advantage of the excellent higher education offered in Britain. I had pursued a Masters in Educational Psychology from the University of Strathclyde and a PhD in Disability Studies from the University of London, Pam had earned a Masters in Special Education from the University of Manchester. I then worked for nine years at the University of Guyana (UG). UG, the only other University in Guyana, accepts students at Grade 11 : they do not need A Levels to enter. As such, a number of international accreditation bodies equate UG 'degrees' to 'Associate Degrees'.

Having worked at UG for almost a decade, I was well aware of its strengths and weaknesses. A clear challenge that UG faces is the lack of international accreditation that their programmes garner overseas. I had helped to arrange for a friend of mine and a 'graduate' of UG, to do a PhD at a University in UK. The very day he was to travel to UK, I received a call from that University asking me to contact the young man as the University had discovered that his 'degree' from UG was, in fact, an Associate Degree and therefore did not grant him entry to a PhD programme.

On another occasion a lady came to see me in tears. She had earned a 'degree' in Psychology from one of the newly declared 'universities' in Guyana. It had cost her several thousand US dollars and taken four years. She travelled to the US with her 'degree papers' only to be told the qualification was not recognised and was worth "zero credits".

Our intention therefore in moving into the arena of tertiary education was to explore developing partnerships with leading Western Universities to ensure that the courses offered at Nations had clear international accreditation.

MAKING A START

Dr. Cameron, a Surgeon from Canada, had come to Guyana many times to train Guyanese doctors. He happened to be in Guyana for the opening of Nations University and was one of the guest speakers, along with the Prime Minister, the Head of International Development from the University of London, and the Deputy Vice-Chancellor of the University of Guyana.

Later that evening he took out his notebook and asked for the process by which we had received permission to open only the second 'University' in Guyana. Dr. Cameron began to take notes as I told him, tongue in cheek, the story, "You get a pot of blue paint and you paint 'Nations University' on the outside wall". 'Nations University' was formed and opened by the Prime Minister in front of 300 dignitaries years before Guyana appointed a National Accreditation Council who would make things more challenging, and indeed more professional, rather than a mere pot of paint.

There are now a number of tertiary institutions in Guyana offering a range of programmes. It is now left to the National Accreditation Council to see which should be registered and accredited. Guyana now has eight 'off shore' medical schools, attracting hundreds of students from Africa and India and locally. In developing 'Nations University' we were determined that any course we would offer would have full international accreditation and equivalency. Our challenge therefore was to form partnerships with leading Western Universities.

A UNIVERSITY FOR THE GLOBAL ERA

We had operated School of Nations for about five years before we moved into the arena of tertiary education. Pam and I remembered well seeing off our sons years earlier at the airport, as they left for Canada to pursue higher education. They were rather too young to leave but, at that time, we really had no option. It was therefore very easy to empathise with other parents of our High School graduates who wanted us to explore bringing quality University education to Guyana, and at a manageable cost. Nations then developed a plan of action to form partnerships and collaborations with leading UK and North American Universities so that our youth did not have to leave Guyana prematurely.

For far too long Guyana has suffered a massive export of its youth. Our hope was that in bringing internationally accredited qualifications to Guyana we could contribute towards keeping our youth in Guyana for a few more years at a critical stage of their development.

We realised to do this it would mean collaborating with various Universities rather than developing tertiary level courses ourselves as such qualifications would have no international currency once a student left Guyana. Nations University would therefore operate through global linkages. The following Table outlines those collaborations.

ABE training session

THE FOLLOWING TABLE OUTLINES THE COURSES OFFERED AT NATIONS

UNDERGRADUATE & POST GRADUATE COURSES (DEGREES)

'Partner'	Year est.	Course(s) offered	# grad.	# in process	Comments
Cambridge International Examination	2001	International Diplomas: Information Technology, Office Procedures, Travel & Tourism & Business	850		These programmes are no longer offered by Cambridge.
Cambridge International Examination	2001	Diploma for Teachers & Trainers	83	350	The Ministry of Education, never approved the course and so the numbers dropped very significantly
Association of Business Executives (ABE) UK	2012	Certificate in Business, Management, Travel & Tourism & Entrepreneurship Levels 4, 5 and 6 Business Management Business Management and Human Resources Business Management and Marketing	418		
University of London: Degrees from External Programme	2005	Sociology, Economics, Business and Banking	12		The degree courses were very heavily loaded with Mathematical content and numbers dwindled dramatically as other British Universities ate into the London market.
University of London	2009	LLB Certificate in Law	15	140	We persevered with the LLB programme from London and we now have about 140 students studying the University of London LLB

Partner	Year	Programme			Comments
Australian Institute of Business	2012	MBA	285	146	By 2018 a total of 567 persons had enrolled on this MBA in Business Administration programme. In 2017 AIB decided to cut ties with their 17 international centres as they looked to more lucrative, On Line, markets.
University of Bedfordshire (UK)	2017	MBA BA One-Year Top Up Degree LLM and (in process) 16 other Masters programmes in areas such as; Psychology, Public Health, Cyber Security, International Journalism, Art and Design, International Development, Banking & Finance and Sociology.		37 In process	We now offer the University of Bedfordshire MBA Business Administration in Guyana with specializations in Oil & Gas Management, Health Management, Human Resource Management and Marketing.
Cambridge International Examination	2016	International Certificate in Educational Leadership		In process	The Ministry of Education has now agreed to partner with Nations in offering this training.
	2011	One Year Pre-Law Programme	140	56	
ACCA Accounting	2017	FIA CAT ACCA Levels 1, 2 & 3 Diploma In Accounting & Business Advanced Diploma in Accounting & Business		In process	We are in the process of re-establishing these programmes
Registered Education Provider of the Project Management Institute (USA)	2017	Certified Associate in Project Management (CAPM) Project Management Professional /PMP		40 In process	

Trainings with Corporations & short courses

Guyana Police Force	2017	Courses designed by Nations staff	135	135 senior police officers have now been trained in the areas of leadership and management. The Police are now looking at a one-year Criminology course that Nations is offering in partnership with ABE UK.
National Energy Agency	2017		15	Emotional Intelligence
Emotional Intelligence				
OSHA compliant courses on Health & Safety	2017	OSHA compliant 10 hour Safety & Health (General Industry)	6	
		OSHA compliant 30 hour Safety & Health (General Industry)	25	
Cyber Security	2018	CyNtelligent, USA	13	
Research Methods	2017	Designed by Nations staff	26	
Distance teaching packages : Diplomas in Special Education, Guidance & Counselling, Primary Maths, English for High Schools		Designed by Nations staff		Upcoming

In developing this Plan of Action we were guided by our discussions with students and parents not only from Nations but from other schools who were faced with the same challenges: where to go for tertiary education?

By far the majority of students in Guyana cannot afford to attend University full time. We therefore offered all our courses in the evenings and at weekends. This may well be one of the most attractive features of the programmes offered at Nations, as it allows students to continue with their full-time jobs which is not always possible at other institutions where courses are offered during the day.

This also allowed us to attract part time teachers of quality. The majority of the teaching staff at Nations is part time. This of course leads to significant savings and allows us to pass on the savings to prospective students. In addition however, we bring lecturers from Trinidad and Tobago to meet specific needs.

In each case the students need to meet the entry requirements laid down by the University offering the courses and the admissions procedure is handled by the overseas institution and not Nations. It has not been difficult to recruit significant numbers to each of our courses. The major recruiting tool is now word of mouth and recommendations made by existing students. Nations' role then is to provide quality teaching, counselling and support to students, ensure high quality physical arrangements, and provision of learning materials. All assessments and examinations are carried out by the partner agency.

Nations is constantly updating its library facilities although a number of our partners offer very comprehensive On-Line libraries as part of the package. Whilst the above scheme may not meet the needs of everyone it appears to be working for hundreds, and now thousands of students.

As noted in the Table above partnering with other Universities is not without its challenges. For example, the degree courses from the University of London were very heavily loaded with mathematical content and student

Nations wins the Carribean Award for Service to Educaton, 2017

Some of the staff at Nations

numbers dwindled dramatically as other British Universities ate into the London market. Similarly in Trinidad and Tobago the University of London lost hundreds of students over a very short period of time.

STRENGTHS

The strengths of the Nations University approach include:
- We are able to introduce new courses in a speedy fashion. For example, we are in the process of introducing 16 new courses at undergraduate and post graduate levels from the University of Bedfordshire in the next eight months.
- Because of the evening and week end mode of delivery we are able to attract significant numbers of students who are working full time. Furthermore this allows us to employ lecturers who are working full time and from overseas
- All of the courses meet very stringent Quality Assurance procedures from the respective Universities.
- We now have the ability to offer a wide range of courses from certificate, diploma, degree and post graduate level

A NEW ERA BECKONS

The Guyana of 2018 is a world away from the Guyana that Pam and I arrived in forty years ago. Guyana has now discovered one of the biggest oil finds in recent history - as such a new Guyana beckons. Clearly, many will benefit from the dramatic discovery. At Nations we decided to position ourselves to offer some of the training in the area of technology that will be required to meet local workforce quotas.

Two years ago my wife had the foresight to begin to develop Nations as a training base in the area of technology. Meetings were held with Exxon Mobil in Houston and with oil companies, Repsol and Tullow at their base in Guyana with the aim of introducing a programme of workforce development for the oil industry in Guyana at Nations University.

I then travelled for three weeks in Trinidad and Canada in search of a partner to develop training programmes in the area of technology. On that trip I met with 17 international organisations, each was better informed of the potential in Guyana than persons here and each agency was interested in signing a MOU, on the spot with Nations University, such was their faith in what Guyana had to offer. We decided on forming a partnership with LearnCorp International (LCI) from Eastern Canada.

In partnership with LCI, the plan is to introduce a two-year technical programme in the areas of mechanical, electrical and process operations. To date, it has been a challenging process to get the oil companies focussed and supporting our proposal. Nevertheless, we plan to proceed anyway by establishing a well-equipped technology workshop and then begin by offering technology courses locally. We have now formed a partnership with Trinizuela, based in Trinidad, to offer City and Guilds training in a number of technology areas. Trinizuela has been offering these courses in Trinidad to thousands of persons for the past 50 years.

Another development is the introduction of University-level courses at our branch of Nations in New Amsterdam, a neighbouring town 60 miles from the capital Georgetown. Furthermore, the Regional Chairman,

the Regional Executive Officer, the local Member of Parliament and the Regional Education Officer of another region, Upper Demerara, invited Nations to offer the University courses at a venue they would provide freely in the hope of offering new opportunities in this depressed area. Efforts are also being made to secure a branch of Nations in Lethem, a town on the Brazilian border. The rationale in expanding into rural areas is simply to offer the Nations courses as widely as possible throughout Guyana; an option that is currently denied to people living outside of the capital.

In addition to the outreach within Guyana, Nations is also looking at international partnerships with like-minded organisations. In November 2017 I travelled to The Gambia to meet with the team at the NGO Starfish and to formulate a partnership with this visionary organisation. Other visits are planned in 2018 to Suriname, Ethiopia, Zambia and South Africa. The rationale for this international expansion is to develop a vision of World Citizenship by fostering partnerships with like-minded agencies.

RESEARCH AND EVALUATION

Research and development is an integral part of third level education as it is the vehicle for gaining new insights and applying new knowledge. With this in mind, Nations invested in developing Nations Research Institute (NURI) – the research and consultancy branch of Nations University.

NURI has a number of strands and functions. It supports development initiatives, but it also undertakes research and information gathering; and provides consultancy advice based on its research.

NURI is an international collaboration of experts in the fields of Education, Disability, Public Health, Management and International Development. These experts come from Guyana and from overseas. NURI's mission is to contribute to the field of development with the aim of ever advancing the quality of lives of people in Guyana and overseas.

The NURI associates have all served in national and international capacities in various forms of development work in Guyana and other parts of the world. NURI brings a multi-faceted approach to development work as well as extensive experience of working for the betterment of humanity.

NURI has developed a set of basic premises which may be summarized as follows:

- The purpose of development is the well-being of people in terms of material, intellectual, social and spiritual fulfilment.
- Man's individual development cannot be fostered in isolation from the institutions and structures of the society. Indeed, it is through commitment to the progress of society that an individual can achieve personal development.
- Effective social and individual progress requires a unified vision of the individual and the society. Such a vision can begin to set in motion social processes that address the material and spiritual aspects of life in a unified way. Together such processes impel development.
- Development therefore, can never be a product that is created outside of a region or a people and then delivered to them. To be effective development can only be envisioned in the context of the participation of people and their institutions, which must consciously tread their own path of individual and social progress.
- Development cannot be a process of simply imitating the so-called 'developed countries'. The very emphasis on the material aspects of those cultures has contributed towards the fragmentation of the moral fabric of the societies, we need therefore to explore new understandings of the term "development".

RESEARCH AND INFORMATION GATHERING

The study that NURI undertook on behalf of UNICEF to provide in-depth information on the knowledge, attitudes and behaviours of youth in Guyana, can illustrate the approach taken by NURI. This was also an example of an international partnership, in this case with Debora Goetz, a gifted researcher from Booz Allen Hamilton, a management consulting firm based in McLean, Virginia, USA. Together with researchers from VF, a questionnaire was developed and administered to 3,436 persons by volunteers on the Youth Can Move the World Programme. The survey explored the respondent's exposure to AIDS educational efforts, level of knowledge about AIDS, and sexually related behaviours. The study then proceeded to make recommendations on prevention efforts in Guyana and suggestions for future survey efforts. The findings were published in a major international journal.

CONSULTANCY

NURI also undertakes a variety of local and international consultancies. This has mainly focused on how advice and recommendations are derived and discussed with commissioning agencies – with an emphasis on clarification of aims and outcomes.

As NURI is based on the contributions of a wide range of professionals it therefore is able to respond to the requirements of a variety of different consultancies in areas such as; disability surveys, Community Based Rehabilitation, Inclusive Education, Literacy, Domestic Violence, Gender Issues, Project Management, Youth Empowerment, Monitoring and Evaluation, Public Health, and Moral Leadership

In recent years NURI has undertaken a range of research projects and consultancies.

In Kosovo, in the Balkans, NURI has undertaken a Situational Analysis on behalf of UNICEF and UNDP on the needs of people with disabilities. Also in Kosovo, NURI undertook the development of a Tempus IV proposal on Higher Education on behalf of the European Union for AAB University.

In 2005 the European Union supported NURI in undertaking a project for training community members in the importance of early stimulation.

In 2008 The First Lady of Guyana encouraged NURI to take on an ILO project on Child Labour.

In 2009 Nuri undertook an evaluation of the contribution of Civil Society in Guyana to the challenge of HIV/AIDs, on behalf of the World Bank

A year later, NURI undertook a disability survey in 12 English speaking countries in the Caribbean on behalf of PAHO/WHO and then formulated a Plan of Action based on these findings.

Over the course of four years, between 2008 to 2012, NURI secured almost half a million US dollars in funding from the European Union in collaboration with Luxembourg Government and Unity Foundation, Luxembourg for the development of the Youth Can Move the World, On the Wings of Words and Community Based Rehabilitation programmes in Guyana.

In 2018 NURI won a US$57,000 contract from US AID for an after-school programme aimed at challenging the propensity for crime in certain identified communities of the capital.

TRIUMPHS AND TRIBULATIONS

ACHIEVEMENTS

We have been successful in de-mystifying research and evaluation and making it more accessible to 'lay' persons.

An integral part of all the innovations has been the promotion of a culture of information gathering, reflection and review.

Nations has endeavoured to interlink research, evaluation and implementation rather than the prevailing notion of seeing them as separate activities. In doing so, Nations has attempted to develop a body of expertise that has been rooted in community development and has come out of a low-income country as opposed to the findings in the literature that come only from the West. We have tried to develop a range of methodologies that have proven to be effective across cultures and topic areas. In the process it has generated a measure of international recognition and sharing of expertise beyond Guyana.

ABE training session

SHORTFALLS

Whatever achievements there have been, they need to be set against an inhospitable environment. There is a clear lack of appreciation among policy makers and funders about the value of research and evaluation.

It should come as no surprise therefore that there is a serious lack of trained personnel in the area of research and development in Guyana. This leads to an over-reliance on a few key individuals and no funds to employ personnel with a remit for research and evaluation.

The Guyana of the 1980s and 1990s was not conducive to research and the sharing of knowledge about the development of the projects. Despite some efforts to do so, insufficient time was given to documenting learning and publishing it internationally. The funders wanted action and this took priority over writing.

Moreover, the scripts of the funders focussed on 'short-termism' projects had to be undertaken quickly and over a short term. Therefore, it was difficult to study the evolution and sustainability of projects beyond three years.

CONCLUSION

It was sobering visiting 17 international organisations in Canada in search of a partner for technology training in light of the oil and gas windfall. Each of the 17 Canadian agencies knew far more re the potential in Guyana than persons in this country. For too long the future tense has been missing in Guyanese conversations.

The hope now is that a new chapter is yet to be written in third level education that will feature a new breed of leader in the field of education and development that will begin to reap the harvest that is on offer.

REFLECTION *by Taslikiyah Stewart-Fox*

I am Nations

The journey at Nations University (NU) for me began 10 years ago when I was asked by a friend to be her replacement as she was offered a scholarship to pursue a Masters. I took the position as Administrative Manager, as in my mind it was a 'low key' job, having just moved back to Guyana from the United States of America. Little did I know at the time, it would be the most exciting, fast-paced yet transformational journey of my life.

In my current capacity of Academic Director, a few months ago, after reflecting on the growth of NU and listening to students' experiences, we decided to market our brand using the slogan 'I am Nations'. The thought behind this is that the qualities NU embraces are qualities that can also make a difference in the individual lives of its stakeholders and ultimately make an impact in the world at large.

NU represents embracing diversity. Students from all walks of life come to our campus seven days a week to pursue programmes from several different universities and institutions based in several different countries. The rich culture and variety adds to enhancing the students' and staff's experiences in and out of the classroom. In a country so divided on political issues, Nations has become a hub for peace and acceptance. I am Nations!

NU represents quality. Quality is at the very core of everything we do. From the facilities, to the lecturers and the administrators, the emphasis is on offering a service that will bridge the gap between students' expectations and students' experience. The Quality Management Team is constantly looking at ways to improve the standards of NU and raise the bar for educational institutions in Guyana. I am Nations!

NU is visionary. Dr. Brian O'Toole and Pam O'Toole have a visible love for Guyana and education and as such have the passion to see enhancement in these areas. Dr. O'Toole relentlessly seeks and pursues partnerships that will bring affordable opportunities in education to Guyanese that may not overwise be possible, while Mrs O'Toole works tirelessly to support his vision. This united effort inevitably trickles down to lower levels and fosters unity amongst staff and students. I am Nations!

NU listens. Nations has an 'open-door' policy where everyone is approachable. Students and lecturers are free to voice concerns and rest assured that their concerns will be dealt with appropriately. Additionally, students are constantly asked to complete student feedback forms to share their views and student representatives are elected to represent the interest of students on an administrative level. This is a welcomed initiative as the culture in Guyana is not one where listening to the customer or the citizen is prevalent and when it is done, very rare does it impact decisions. I am Nations!

The epitome of Nations!
A few years ago, Dr. O'Toole and I met with a 32-year-old man who was keen on pursuing law after having dropped out of high school. We both fully supported his vision and shifted timetables and arranged for private tutoring to help the young man to complete the exam that our 5th Form students sit, International General Certificate of Secondary Education (IGCSE). After succeeding in his exams, we then arranged for him to receive the support needed to sit the Advanced Level examinations. A few months later, he walked into my office with his A Levels results and his application form to pursue his LLB. He is now in the final stages of completing his LLB from the University of London offered through Nations University. Our goal is to help every individual to pursue their dreams despite their background. This is the epitome of Nations! I am Nations!

CHAPTER 7 CONCLUSION

REFLECTIONS
ON A ROAD LESS TRAVELLED

Brian O'Toole

This book began with an overview of what Guyana was like in 1977 when our adventure with the country began. In proposing marriage to my wife 40 years ago, I told her there were precious few possibilities for professional advancement in a country that was only 'beaten' by Haiti to earn the accolade of one of the poorest countries in all of the Americas. And then, fast forward 40 years later, and the announcement is made that the biggest oil deposits in the world have now been found in that same land.

A few months ago, I attended a meeting, along with 300 others, in one of the top hotels in the capital as the former Minister of Natural Resources in Trinidad and Tobago, shared the history of recent oil finds across the world. He stated, very clearly, that Guyana would be transformed even within the next two or three years. Whether we would learn from the experience of Angola, Guinea Bissau, Nigeria, Mozambique and indeed our neighbour, Trinidad and Tobago or whether we would have the courage, vision and leadership to create a modern-day, oil and gas success story would depend, in no small part, on the actions of many of the persons gathered in that room.

More than at any time in our history we cry out for a cadre of leaders to be inspired, honest and visionary. We will not have to wait too long to see if history has been kind to Guyana in this respect. Guyana, with almost zero expertise and experience in oil and gas now sits down at a 'bargaining' table with the giants of EXXON Mobil, Repsol, Tullow and other major energy players. What kind of leadership is now required in Guyana? This book has attempted to suggest some paths that could be explored, albeit on roads less travelled.

It is all too easy, with the benefit of hindsight, to present the various interventions outlined in this book as a coherent plan and gloss over the many challenges that were faced on the way. What have been some of the key lessons to come out of this journey? A key contribution of the interventions outlined in this book was the nurturing of certain key principles many of which required a culture shift to be put into operation.

COMMUNITY EMPOWERMENT

Any intervention needs to be based on a profound respect for the community. The key to achieving this is the practice of open and equitable consultation as an integral part of the development process. We tried to put this into effect in the meetings we had throughout the interior and coastal regions of Guyana to take time to listen at community meetings where villagers voiced their concerns and needs.

At the same time however, it is all too easy to paint a rosy picture of village communities where there is harmony and a united vision. The reality is often much different. There is a great danger that in reflecting on our development efforts we neglect to point out the struggles. There is no shame in admitting one's problems. Indeed, it would be naïve to expect that such innovations would be immune from disunity and jealousies.

One of the most sobering challenges on this journey was trying to deal with resentment from unlikely quarters and from persons that we expected to be our allies. But, as the programmes grew, we attracted resentment rather than a sense of shared pride. A key skill that needs to be developed in such situations is how to manage change and how to cope with such negativity. No doubt, more could have been done to encourage persons to walk this path with us, to seek their guidance and involvement and share with them our thoughts, plans and progress.

CHANGE TAKES TIME

We need to appreciate that change in development terms takes time and often involves a transformation in human values. International funding agencies, in their desire to placate their masters in New York, Stockholm and London, however adopt totally unrealistic time frames. The challenge becomes how to cope with the indecent haste of major funders who require speedy results to be uploaded into their Logical Frameworks as reports to their demanding seniors.

There is a danger in such projects that one underestimates the stress that is created by introducing change. At the heart of this project was the challenge to introduce a new way of looking at things on the part of the key government workers in the community.

A major concern therefore was how to stay positive amidst such conditions. We drew strength however from a profound respect for the Guyanese people and the clear belief that they had the capacity to bring about and indeed lead fundamental change in their own condition.

A major challenge is how to respond when motivation and enthusiasm runs out. The inputs of the key persons in each of the chapters highlight the crucial role that the animators and regional coordinators play in keeping the projects alive. Moreover, we have to take time to listen to the intended 'consumers' both during the implementation of the programme as well as at the outset. We need to get to know them and to begin to see the world through their eyes.

NEED FOR ON-GOING REFLECTION

The chapter on the "On the Wings of Words" programme highlights the crucial role played by the quarterly 'Look Back, Step Ahead' meetings where the participants were invited to come together to reflect on challenges, explore responses and ensure that the intervention remained true to its goals and objectives. All too often however we say 'we are too busy to do this.'

LEADERSHIP THROUGH PARTNERSHIPS

At the heart of this process was the attempt to articulate a new model of leadership, that of Servant Leadership, based on systems change and fanning grassroots initiatives. A key aspect of the project was the attention given to promoting the spiritual principles which should guide the intervention. This included the collaborative nature of the initial design of the project, attention to the empowerment of the local population at the grassroots, the focus on consultation throughout and the overriding principle of trust and faith in the capacity of those being served.

This book reflects on the need for a new model of educational leadership. We have attempted to illustrate one contribution towards this goal by creating a new style of working, through partnerships. We believe, such an approach will be far more profitable than pursuing traditional hierarchical management systems.

We were buoyed in this by developing effective partnerships with a number of organisations. Health for Humanity (HH) was one of these partners. But, this too, presented its challenges as some within HH were still tied to a concept of development based on what could be donated in terms of equipment and supplies rather than embracing a more searching model of intervention based on empowerment and support of local initiatives. For some of the highly trained medical experts from HH, it was difficult to play the role of 'the wind in the sails' when they had been accustomed for so long to taking the tiller and guiding the process.

A deeper understanding is required of the potential inherent in North/South partnerships and more reflection is required concerning how best to prepare the Western 'experts' for the new role they are being asked to play.

All too often development projects are executed as if in a vacuum. If the community is not involved any gains will be piecemeal and short lived. In the chapter on CBR we learnt of the role of Primary Health Care workers advising the family in their homes, the role that regular teachers need to play to create a more welcoming environment for children with special needs within the regular school, and the key role of local businesses in opening their doors to offer real work.

The chapters on CBR and the Bahá'í Community Health Partnership highlight the crucial role to be played by elected committees from the community. The challenge then becomes how to support and nurture these committees so that services survive beyond the set-up phase.

AVOIDANCE OF DEPENDENCY

An overriding consideration has been the need to avoid the creation of dependency and seek to promote sustainability. The Bahá'í Community Health Partnership in the interior of Guyana began with a clearly stated goal of phasing itself out within a decade. The intervention was based on the recognition that local communities should be encouraged and trained to assume responsibility for as much of the project as possible.

COMMITMENT AND DEDICATION

As small NGOs, Varqa Foundation and Nations Research Institute (NURI) were able to hand-pick key staff for qualities of flexibility, commitment and for their people skills. The challenge then becomes, how to incorporate these small scale innovations into existing government systems in the hope of greatly expanding the coverage. However, the reality of most government systems is that they are plagued by poor pay and conditions, low morale, limited receptivity, and low energy. The CBR chapter illustrates this with the very different results achieved by volunteers as compared with government school teachers.

What therefore is the role of government in such development initiatives? The role can include; enacting legislation, establishing for example a National Council for Disability, or assigning ministerial responsibility for such issues and the establishment of national standards for services.

NEW MODELS OF TRAINING

At the heart of any of these interventions is quality training. We simply need to get better at training. We constantly need to reflect on whether the training we offer meets the needs of the participants. One way to achieve the goal of sustainability was to put knowledge transfer at the heart of the programme.

RESOURCES

 An ironic challenge in the depleted economy of Guyana in the early 1980s, was to resist the seduction of major funders, who in a bid to spend their allocated budgets offered far more resources than in fact were required. For example, when we approached the European Union for funding we were informed that we had to greatly increase the budget or the programme would not be funded.

There is also a real danger that funders take a domineering role and indeed fund the project at a level that makes sustainability impossible from the outset. A real challenge to the pioneers of such programmes is the danger of getting seduced by the magnitude of funding that is floated by the development agencies. Rather, in programmes like On the Wings of Words, we attempted to demonstrate what could be achieved with only moderate amounts of funds.

All the programmes outlined in this book highlight what can be achieved once we effectively mobilise the greatest resource that a country such as Guyana possesses – its people.

I had the opportunity to undertake a series of consultancies on CBR for various UN agencies. In almost every country I visited a challenging issue was always 'who' would provide the service? The pioneers of the WHO approach (Helander et al, 1989) look to Community Health Workers and others within the government system as the key service providers. The reality often however was that such poorly paid workers resented more responsibilities.

Moreover, in many countries finding 'volunteers' was very difficult, if not impossible. By contrast this was never a problem in Guyana and the programmes outlined here. It may not be a coincidence that Guyana has not yet been spoilt by the plethora of international aid agencies operating throughout the poorer parts of the world who almost vie with each other to secure the services of key community workers. On five visits to Ghana, for example, I saw such agencies outbidding one another to get the best resources from the community. The services that villagers had offered freely for hundred of years were now on sale in the market place to the highest bidder.

The danger can also become that more time is spent applying for grants than in doing the work. Almost all the interventions outlined in this book, with the exception of School of Nations, are supported by external funding. The challenge then becomes how can such programmes ever be owned by the community when they are reliant on external funding and subject to the priorities set by the funders?

Going forward there may need to be new negotiations for donor funding and insisting that government develop joint projects which have been developed through consultation with local communities. Funding needs to be phased so that it gradually tapers off.

IN DEVELOPMENT WHO SHOULD SET THE AGENDA?

There is a real danger that funders dictate the priorities for the community. Over the years NURI has undertaken a wide range of development projects on behalf of ILO, World Bank, WHO, UNICEF and US AID. Each year or two, the focus of these agencies appears to change from child labour to disability, from crime prevention to HIV/AIDs. It may be time to question who is setting the agenda for these interventions? Are we responding to the felt need of the community or is the focus defined by 'experts' thousands of miles away?

The chapter on the Rupununi illustrates this point. From the first visit to this very remote region, on the border with Brazil, it was clear that disability, the focus of the AIFO funded CBR programme, was not in any way a perceived need of the Rupununi community. Instead of challenging this analysis the CBR team began by addressing the identified needs of the community, in terms of early child development and the promotion of literacy. Indeed, it was several years before the CBR intervention again introduced disability as a focus to the intervention. But by that stage the CBR team had won the respect of the community and the villagers themselves began to explore what could be done for the disabled persons in the region who, up to that point, had not 'existed.' If, however, AIFO had not facilitated that very patient (and expensive) 'preamble' we would never had been able to see what could be done in an impoverished indigenous community to meet the needs of persons with disabilities in their midst.

The CBR Programme therefore evolved into an empowering process in this isolated Amerindian region which went far beyond the usual definition of rehabilitation by affirming indigenous culture and putting the process of development back into the hands of the community.

Rehabilitation was now addressed within the wider context of community issues through an integration into existing infrastructure and the education of parents and community members rather than a top down model of service delivery. The focus became the empowerment of the community to care for their children with disabilities.

NEED FOR INTEGRATED MODELS OF DEVELOPMENT

The new mantra of developers is "to enable communities to help themselves". In the area of disability this will require a paradigm shift from 'rehabilitation' to a focus on 'community' and an exploration of where such services should be located. WHO was largely unsuccessful in more than 15 years of attempts to locate the CBR workers within the health system.

At the heart of any intervention also needs to be the recognition that economic independence is the key need. NURI was recently approached by a major donor to undertake an after-school programme for children and youth in vulnerable, high crime risk, communities. The agenda for the intervention had been fixed by 'experts' from overseas. The focus was to be on art, music and drama. It took several meetings with the funding agency before we were 'allowed' to include entrepreneurship training as a key part of the intervention and as a means of income generation so as to help lift the young people out of poverty.

WHAT IS THE PLACE OF SPIRITUALITY IN DEVELOPMENT?

When I travel in Europe or North America I am very quickly made to realise that the fastest way to stop a conversation is to talk about 'spiritual issues.' Many of the chief architects of international development come from those same backgrounds. UNICEF informed Varqa Foundation, a Bahá'í inspired agency, that they were unable to fund copies of the Youth Can Move the World manual as one section focused on the use of the Ruhi materials for social and community transformation. The Ruhi materials have now been in use in more than 75 countries throughout the world over the past 30 years. Fortunately, the Office of Social and Economic Development at the Bahá'í World Centre in Israel offered seed money to VF to ensure that the Ruhi course did indeed form a key part of the intervention. To respect UNICEF, two separate manuals were therefore produced for the YCMTW programme, one with social issues and the arts, sponsored by UNICEF, and the other with the Ruhi materials funded by the international Bahá'í community.

At the heart of this spiritual foundation is the belief that ordinary people in the community should be the key players in these development initiatives. Family members, neighbours and school teachers are available throughout the world. The challenge then becomes how to mobilise, accompany, support and nurture these key resources.

A key guiding principle throughout this journey has been the inspiration and guidance that Pam and I receive as members of the Bahá'í Faith. However, that has not been without its own challenges, as some of the strongest critics came from those closest to us.

JOURNEY'S END?

It has been a journey of 40 years. Pam and I arrived in a country that was regarded as one of the poorest in the entire region and now we see the early signs of oil discoveries that could transform this small nation. To take advantage of this new wealth needs a new code of moral leadership that will chart a course of development that may inspire others. Presently few in Guyana are optimistic about this scenario. For our own part we remain committed to a bright and exciting future and we are thankful that Guyana has been our home and that it offers such potential for fundamental change and development.

In this 40-year journey, we have had the privilege of working with a number of truly exceptional people, a number of them have offered their insights in this book. The hope now is that others may seek some inspiration from their efforts in terms of what can be achieved in, what in 1978 appeared to be a very daunting context in which to work. Guyana is in dire need of a new generation of community activists and animators.

In the words of Bahá'u'lláh, "Mount your steeds O heroes of God!"

REFLECTION *by*
Emeritus Professor Roy McConkey
on International aid and community development

International aid from affluent countries of the north to the poorest ones of the south is a multi-billion dollar enterprise. Although it has had brought significant gains in terms of poverty alleviation, better health care and improved educational systems, there have been notable failings, principally in terms of value for money. The government-to-government approach has fallen foul of bureaucracy, corruption, poor governance and unsustainable projects which has resulted in protracted delays in improving the lives of ordinary citizens and especially those who are most marginalised.

The chapters of this book have described a radically different approach to international aid that depends on friendships more than finance, on commitment more than contracts and on perseverance more than prestige. Brian and Pam O'Toole came to Guyana with arguably the greatest gift a donor can bring: a commitment to live among the people they aimed to serve for as long as they were needed. Forty years later it is still their home. Their work is not finished and probably never will be.

Their greatest legacy is not so much the tangible programmes described in these pages, impressive as they are. Rather it is the manner in which the O'Tooles worked. Three key elements contributed to successful outcomes. First, their endeavours were rooted in a deep appreciation and understanding of Guyanese cultures and practices. They took time to build relationships across all strata of society. Their personal engagement in local settings was vital to building trust despite the long journeys and personal hardships it entailed. They listened respectfully to people's concerns and constraints. They soon appreciated that Western theories and strategies had to be refined, reconstructed and even abandoned so that relevant interventions could flourish in Guyana.

Second, they strove to empower local personnel to solve their problems. They recognised and harnessed the creative talents of local personnel and through a combination of knowledge sharing and the production of tangible resources, made it possible for local communities to support one another in making life better and more meaningful for everyone. The old adage of: 'give a man a fish and you feed him for a day: teach a man to fish and you feed him for a lifetime' was brought to life in the villages of Guyana.

Third, they persevered despite the set-backs, jealousies, competing priorities, personnel shortages and lack of funds. Not for them a short-term secondment or consultancy. They were in for the long haul which required both determination and optimism as well as dedication from them. Yet their leadership qualities that are so essential to community development, are ones that no management degree can teach or consultancy firm will engender. Brian and Pam literally put their heart and soul into every facet of their work. That's what made the difference.

In one sense, the O'Toole's approach to community development is neither original nor unique. Recent history recounts similar efforts by brave adventurers who chose to leave their homelands and bring betterment to people in distance lands. Indeed it's likely that the affluent countries of today also gained from well-intended foreigners who brought new ways of thinking and acting. Given such a long tradition allied to its evident success, it is all the more puzzling that international aid remains dominated by a 'top-down', managerial approach. That is not to say that one is always better than the other. More likely both are needed, but for this to happen greater cognisance has to be paid to nurturing the personnel and the skills they need to implement what could be called 'bottom-up' approaches. This book provides a clear illustration and model that community developers of the future will hopefully emulate so that the road they take is no longer, less travelled.

Students from Tiger Bay

Gordon Naylor

Dr. Farzin Rahmani
with Dr. O'Toole

Dr. Soma Stout

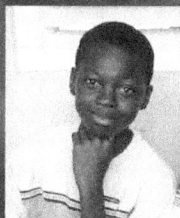

MBA Graduation 2017

Dr. Rustom Behesti

INDEX

REFERENCES

Arbab, F (1992) 'Development – a challenge to Bahá'í scholars,' Bahá'í Studies Notebook, 3:1-19

Anello, E (2001) 'Moral Leadership,' European Business Forum

Bahá'í International Task Force on Literacy (1989) Bahá'í World Centre, Israel

Chapman (1998) private correspondence, European Union

Friere, P (2000) 'Pedagogy of the Oppressed,' New York, Continuum

Guyana Education Access Project (1998) Screening tests to identify children with special needs.

Hargreaves,A and Fullan, M (2012) 'Professional Capital- Transforming Teaching in Every School,' Teachers College, Columbia University

Helander,E, Mendis,P. Nelson, G and Goerdt,A (1989) 'Training the Disabled in the Community,' Geneva, Switzerland

Hoffmans T and de Roos V (1995) 'A Decade of Hopeful Steps in Guyana – a participatory, comprehensive evaluation of the CBR programme in Guyana,' University of Limburg, The Netherlands

Holt, J (1964), 'How children fail,' Pitman

Jennings, R. (1994) 'Assessment of literacy levels,' University of Guyana

Miles,M (1985) 'Where there is no Rehab plan, Peshawar, Pakistan

Miles J and and Pierre L (1994) 'Offering Hope: a report on an evaluation of Guyana's CBR programme for Disabled children,' AIFO, Italy

One Country Magazine (2005) Vol 17, Issue #2, 'In Guyana, young people take the lead in an effort to avoid risky behaviours.'

One Country Magazine (1998) 'In Guyana, the use of moral "generative themes" propels a project for youth.'

O'Toole,B (1989) 'An evaluation of the Guyana CBR programme', PhD Institute of Education, University of London

O'Toole,B, McConkey R, Goetz D (2007) 'Knowledge and attitudes of young people in Guyana to HIV/AIDS,' International Journal of STD & AIDS, Vol 18, pp 193-197

O'Toole, B and Goetz D C (2003), 'HIV/AIDS Questionnaire Survey Results,' Varqa Foundation, Guyana

UNDP (2016) Human Development Report, Human Development for Everyone

UNICEF (2016) Situational Analysis of children and Women in Guyana', UNICEF, Guyana

UNESCO (1988) 'Understanding and Responding to Children's Needs in Inclusive Classrooms,' UNESCO, Paris

UNICEF `Facts for Life: a communications challenge,' DIPA, New York

Publications by Dr. Brian O'Toole

1987: 'Community Based Rehabilitation: Problems and Possibilities.' European Journal of Special Needs Education, Vol 2 No 3, 177 – 190, (1987).

1988: 'CBR Reaching the Unreached.' International Journal of Special Education, Vol 3, No 1, 21 – 37, (1988).

1988: 'An Evaluation of a Community Based Rehabilitation Programme in Guyana.' International Journal of Rehabilitation Research, Vol 11 (4), 323 – 334 (1988).

1989: 'Step by Step: A Community Based Rehabilitation Programme for Disabled Children in Rural Areas of Guyana' World Health Forum, Vol 10 238 – 239, (1989).

1989: 'The Relevance of Parental Involvement Programmes in Developing Countries.' Child Care, Health and Development, Vol 15, 1 – 15 (1989). Reprinted in the International Journal of Special Education, Vol 4 (2), 173 – 183 (1989).

1990: 'New Directions to Meeting the Challenge of Disability in the 1990's.' In Thorburn M.J. and Marfo. (Eds.) Practical Approaches to Childhood Disability in Developing Countries. Memorial University of Newfoundland.

1990: 'Annotated Bibliography on Community Based Rehabilitation.' In Thorburn M.J. and Marfo K. op. cit. (1990).

1990: 'A Guide to Community Based Services.' Guides for Special Education, No 8, UNESCO, Paris. Translated into French, Spanish, Farsi, Arabic and Portuguese.

1990: 'Rural Rehabilitation in Guyana.' Notes, Comments, Series, 1990, UNESCO, Paris.

1991: 'Community Involvement in Rehabilitation Programmes for Disabled Children – A Guyanese Experience.' Community Development Journal, Vol 26, No 3, 202-209, 1991.

1993: 'Community Based Rehabilitation,' Chapter 13 in the World Yearbook on Education, Kogan Page Publishers, Edited by Peter Mittler, 1993.

1993: 'Community Based Rehabilitation: Video Programmes.' Early Development and Parenting, Vol 1, No 2, 1993.

1993: 'Community based participation: Rehabilitation rooted in the Community,' chapter # 10 in ' The Handicapped Community,' ed H. Finkenflugel, 1993 University of Amsterdam Press.

1993: 'Production of training materials for CBR Programme in Guyana,' chapter # 15 in Finkenflugel (op cit)

1994: 'Community Based Rehabilitation and development: disabled children in Guyana.' Development in Practice, Vol 4, #1, pp 23-24, 1994.

1994: 'Development of training materials for CBR workers in Guyana,' International Journal of Disability, Development and Education (Australia), Vol 42,

1994: 'Involvement of volunteers, parents and community members with children with special needs,' chapter # 4 in 'Examples of good practice in Special Needs Education and CBR Programmes,' UNESCO, 1994.

1994 : O'Toole B and O'Toole P 'Literacy as a means of empowerment,' Chap #12 in World Book of Education

1995: 'Innovations in Developing countries for People with Disabilities,' Eds Brian O'Toole and Roy McConkey, Lisieux Hall Publications. This is an edited collection of over 30 chapters from experts on disability from throughout the world. July, 1995.

1997: 'Where there is no nursery school – one response to the challenge in the interior of Guyana,' O'Toole B and Stout S, pp45-54 in 'First Steps – stories on inclusion in Early Childhood Education, UNESCO

1998 'A training strategy for personnel working in developing countries'. O'Toole, B. & McConkey, R. International Journal of Rehabilitation Research, 21 (3) 311-321.

1999: 'Educating teachers in developing countries about disabilities', McConkey, R., O'Toole, B. & Mariga, L. Exceptionality Education Canada, 9, 15-38.

2000: 'Improving the quality of life of people with disabilities in least affluent countries: Insights from Guyana, South America'. McConkey, R. & O'Toole. In K.D. Keith & R.L. Schalock (eds.) Cross-cultural perspectives on quality of life. Washington DC: American Association on Mental Retardation.

2002: `The challenge of children and adolescents with disabilities in the Caribbean,' pp 63-85 in 'Children's Rights, Caribbean Realities,' Ed. C. Barrow (2002), Randle Publishers.

2003: 'HIV/AIDS Questionnaire Survey Results, funded by UNICEF to provide information on knowledge, attitudes & behavior of youth in Guyana,' by O'Toole & Goetz, UNICEF

2007: 'Knowledge and attitudes of young people in Guyana to HIV/AIDS', O'Toole, B., McConkey, R., Casson, K. Goetz-Goldberg, D. and Yazdani. A. (2007)International Journal of STD & AIDS, 18(3), 193-197.

In Memory of
Rebequa Murphy who told us
years ago that the harvest was
yet to come at Nations

www.ingramcontent.com/pod-product-compliance
Lightning Source LLC
LaVergne TN
LVHW051117080426
835510LV00018B/2097